Salt Dough

Sarah Crosland

The Art of Crafts

First published in 1998 by
The Crowood Press Ltd
Ramsbury, Marlborough
Wiltshire SN8 2HR

© Sarah Crosland 1998

British Library Cataloguing in Publication Data

A catalogue record for this book is available from the British Library.

ISBN 1 86126 129 2

Typeset by Annette Findlay
Printed in China

Contents

Introduction

Salt dough is the medium used in dough crafting and has become very popular for the DIY craft enthusiast because it is economical, easily available and can be adapted to everyone's individual ability. The tools and ingredients are found in most kitchens and you don't need to buy a lot of expensive specialist equipment before you can start on a project. Some modelling skills and an eye for dimension and shape are advantageous but not always necessary, and although there are no hard-and-fast rules to making salt dough, there are some guidelines which I have set out in the following pages to help you. The creative possibilities of salt dough as a modelling medium are endless and the dough can be made by a child into a simple gift or by a skilled craftsperson into an intricate piece of art.

AN ANCIENT CRAFT

The origins of salt dough have been traced back as far as the ancient Egyptians, Greeks and Romans. We know that the strong symbolism connected to salt, flour and water probably prompted the ancients to use these three ingredients as part of their ritualistic ceremonies. Bread represented the four elements of fire, air, earth and water, and played an important part in the worship of mother nature, fertility and harvest. One of the earliest references to bread is in the Old Testament, Genesis 3: 19, when God banished Adam from Eden after he had eaten from the tree of knowledge.

Bread provided life and was the most basic part of all staple diets; the growing and harvesting of cereals was of great importance because the failure of a crop would bring the threat of famine, hardship and death. Ancient cultures used cereals as currency and a good harvest would mean that a country's commercial and trading powers would be secure. Salt was also a highly prized commodity because of its preserving and seasoning powers. The modern word salary is derived from the Latin *salarium* and referred to the payments made to Roman soldiers for the purchase of salt. It was also a custom in Roman times to offer newlyweds a cake made of flour and salt to bring them luck.

Ceres, the Latin form of the great goddess also known as Demeter, was an Olympian deity worshipped by the ancient Greeks and later by the Romans. Ceres, the goddess of corn and harvest, represented mother earth and ruled Rome in the 'lost' period of four centuries before 200BC, a period whose written records were later destroyed by patriarchal historians, leaving only vague information on myths and religious customs.

Farmers viewed Ceres as the protector of their livelihood and kept her rites faithfully for fear of their crops failing. Even Christian farmers worshipped her as recently as in the 19th century in the British Isles, performing a ceremony in the middle of June in which they would walk around their crops with burning torches in memory of Cerealia, hoping to ensure a plentiful harvest.

In India, bread figures are made as lucky talismans to ensure that the following harvest will be a good one. In contrast, the Mexicans bury bread figures with their dead in the hope that they will ensure immortality.

There are references to salt dough in the folklore and art of many European countries. We know that when the tradition of having a tree at Christmas was

started in the 19th century in northern Europe, salt dough was commonly used to make decorations, the high salt content protecting the decorations from vermin. In Scandinavia, dough crafting has been popular for many years and fine examples of work and information about the craft have come from this part of the world.

European immigrants who travelled and settled in America in the 17th century took with them many of their traditional crafts. These were derived from the most basic of materials and the need of often poor minority communities to reassert the ethnic tradition, folklore and customs of their mother countries. The revival of folk art in America in recent years has meant that there is a huge interest in doughcraft, which is sometimes known as clay dough. I have often come across people whose first introduction to salt dough has been through either a visit to the States or a gift brought back by a friend.

Nowadays, although the more traditional designs are still very popular, there is a more contemporary feel to many dough artists' work as they experiment with the medium, using it instead of clay or papier mâché to make bowls, vases, candlestick holders, picture frames and jewellery.

Being a traditionalist at heart, I still love the natural look of the dough and many of my designs are influenced by nature and what I see around me. You will notice that I have a special fondness for dough fruit and flowers, plain unpainted rings and the friendly jolly faces of dough dollies. In fact, I was first introduced to salt dough by a friend who had made a batch of dough dollies for her daughter's birthday party. They were lying on a cooling rack waiting to be painted and quite honestly looked good enough to eat. I was very intrigued by the recipe and baking method, and, having always enjoyed modelling with clay, I decided to have a go at making some dough dollies for my children. After several attempts, the results of which resembled small bricks with arms and legs and weighed almost as much, I started to get the hang of it and soon every flat surface in our small terraced cottage was covered with dough! My family got used to eating salads and convenience food as the oven was always full of dough, and nobody dared open the oven door on pain of death!

Having exhausted the supply of friends and family I could give dough models to for birthdays, Christmases and other festive occasions, I decided to take a basketful of dough models to my local craft shop. The owner kindly put them in her shop window and we agreed to market them on a commission basis. They did not take long to sell and she was soon taking orders for personalized dough dollies and rings with fruit and flowers on them. By the end of the first year in salt dough production I had built up a network of retail outlets as far afield as Hampshire and Cumbria. I relied on friends and relations to transport my dough around the country; I have a very good friend who worked for a duck processing factory in Lincolnshire who discovered that the ladies in her office and on the factory floor loved doughcraft; she was soon holding dough parties at her house and getting orders for me to produce.

As my knowledge and skill in doughcraft improved, I was asked by my local education authority to give talks and demonstrations in the craft. I found that children really enjoyed modelling, especially when it meant getting covered in flour and making a mess. The versatility of the medium meant that it did not matter if mistakes were made during the modelling stage, because they could always start again without damaging the dough or wasting the ingredients. This made it a good alternative to plasticine, fimo or modelling clay.

Through my time spent exhibiting at craft fairs, running doughcraft courses and writing about the craft, I have been amazed at the diversity of people interested in the craft. It has grown from being something that people associated with primary school to being an acceptable medium for sugarcraft artists, cake decorators, bakers, pastry cooks and potters to diversify into.

SAFETY WITH SALT DOUGH, CHILDREN AND PETS

Although the dough is an organic substance, the high salt content and the fact that we mix into it wallpaper adhesive, which contains fungicides, can make it irritating to the skin. As children love playing with the dough, make sure that they do not rub their eyes with salty fingers or try to eat the dough, although I can almost guarantee that they will not

try it more than once as it tastes quite horrible! A greedy Labrador I know gobbled down some unvarnished dough fruit, which he obviously thought were dog biscuits and quite delicious at the time. Unfortunately he was driven mad with thirst and kept his owner up all night asking to be let out into the garden because he had then drunk so much water.

If you are planning to sell your work, check that the paints you are using are toysafe, that is, they are not harmful if swallowed; most paint manufacturers label their products with health and safety logos. Always use solvent-based paints and varnishes in a well ventilated room, and keep them away from small children.

1 The Tools

The most important tools needed for modelling the dough arc your fingers. Other tools can range from the most basic kitchen equipment used for baking or bread-making to an array of cookie cutters, cake decorators' piping nozzles, sugarcraft cutters and artists' paints and brushes. Through trial and error I have discovered the artistic potential of a garlic crusher or a lemon zester, and my star-shaped icing nozzle has hardly ever been used for cakes since I found that it made beautiful star-burst patterns on dough. I have made the list of those tools which are essential and do not need an explanation, and those that I have adapted and can be used to create special effects and finishes for each of the projects that follow.

FOR MAKING THE DOUGH

- Weighing scales
- Measuring jug
- Mixing bowl
- Wooden spoon
- Rubber gloves

FOR MODELLING AND BAKING

Silicon Baking Parchment

This non-stick baking paper is better than greaseproof paper or aluminium foil for lining the baking tray. The models do not stick and the paper can be re-used many times. It also helps to model directly onto a square of paper so that you can move the model about and lift it easily onto the baking tray.

Flat Baking Tray

Baking trays become rusty after constant use with salt dough even when lined with parchment, so buy a cheap one and keep it just for the dough.

Oven Temperature Gauge

This is essential if you are not sure about the oven settings on your cooker. No two ovens are the same and if you are in doubt this gadget will tell you exactly what temperature your oven is set at.

Rolling Pin

A rolling pin with a revolving barrel is ideal for rolling out sheets of dough. The dough is put under stress when it is rolled and the revolving barrel helps to spread the pressure evenly on the dough. Children's play dough rolling pins are handy for using on small pieces of dough.

Pastry Brush or Small Paintbrush

I find that using a paintbrush instead of a pastry brush is easier for joining small pieces of dough with water.

Small Sharp Knife

This is essential for cutting dough, using around stencils and templates, veining leaves and marking fruit.

Plastic-Covered Horticultural Training Wire

This thin wire makes a very good hanging loop, and can be found at garden centres. The plastic coating protects the wire from the corrosive damage from the salt and will last for years. It will also withstand temperatures of up to 150°C. It will bend into any shape and is ideal for rings and wreaths, giving added support at the joins. A small pair of pliers is necessary for cutting the wire.

Paperclips

These make suitable hanging hooks for small models.

Cookie Cutters/Sugarcraft Cutters

These are available in plastic or metal, in an assortment of shapes and sizes. For the projects that follow you will need a set of leaf cutters and a set of blossom cutters.

FOR DECORATIVE EFFECTS

Small Sharp Scissors

An old pair of nail scissors makes an ideal tool for making ears of corn, the spines on a hedgehog, fish scales or even hair. Make sure that you wash and dry them thoroughly after use.

Lemon Zester

This handy gadget produces beading around picture frames and clothes when it is pressed into the dough.

Garlic Press

This can be used for making an array of different finishes including curly hair, grass, straw, fleece, manes and tails. Individual strands can be used to make delicate flower stems or tiny wreaths.

Cheese or Nutmeg Grater

For making the pitted skins on an orange, or adding texture to a basket.

Fine Metal Sieve

For making fine hair and grass.

Plastic Icing Nozzles

The various patterns that these can produce when pressed into the dough can be quite inspirational. Use them to create star patterns, or push some coloured dough through one and make small round bushes and trees. Always dip the

nozzle in flour before pressing it into the dough, or it will stick.

Small Forks

Two small forks, when held back to back, can be used to press a pattern in the dough resembling the wicker texture of a basket.

Cloves/Twigs/Alder Cones

Cloves make excellent calyces and stalks on apples, pears and oranges. Small pieces of twig can be used for stems on plums, peaches and grapes. Longer twigs can be used to make the trunks of small trees. If you are lucky enough to live near an alder tree, the cones from this tree can be used as miniature fir cones. They can all be added to your models before baking and will not come to any harm in the oven as long as the temperature is kept at 100°C, gas mark ½.

Small Brass Cup Hooks

These are used for making key hangers and are pushed into the dough models before baking.

Cotton Sugarcraft Stamens

Black stamens make very good cherry stalks.

Cocktail Sticks

Wooden cocktail sticks can be used for pressing patterns into dough and adding support to larger models and figures.

FOR COLOURING/PAINTING AND VARNISHING

Food Colours

These are mixed into the dough before modelling and baking.

Sandpaper

Fine or medium grade sandpaper can be used to sand any rough edges off the baked model.

Artists' Decorative Paints

For full description see page 42.

Artists' Paintbrushes

Brushes numbering from 00 to 5, sable- or nylon-tipped, and a couple of broad flat-tipped brushes are all suitable.

Palette or Plate

A palette is not essential: an old plate will do for mixing your paints.

Water Pot or Jam Jar

Used for holding the water to clean your brushes in and mix paints with.

Absorbent Kitchen Paper

Essential for drying your brushes and mopping up spills.

Cotton Wool Buds

These are useful for blending colours together on the dough, and for mopping up excess paint and water on the model.

Spirit-Based Polyurethane Varnish/Water Colour Varnish

These are necessary to preserve your work. There is a full description on page 43.

Soft Varnishing Brushes

You will need a medium-size brush for larger areas and a small paintbrush for fiddly pieces.

Wire Cake Cooling Rack

This is a good way to dry your models once they have been varnished, as it allows you to varnish both sides at the same time. Unfortunately, you will never be able to use your cooling tray for cakes again! If you are just varnishing one or two models, then they can be done one side at a time, resting on a piece of newspaper.

White Spirit

It will be necessary to clean your brushes after use, for which white spirit or a suitable brush cleaner will do.

2 Making the Dough

Making and kneading the dough is a very important part of dough crafting and anyone who enjoys baking and making bread will find this stage easy. Once the dough is made it has to be kneaded for about ten minutes; this stage is essential, however tempting it might be to cheat! I always compare it to a twenty-minute work-out in the gym. The end result is well worth the effort, and the most important point of all is that it will minimize the risk of the dough cracking after it has been baked. The kneading process has a very tactile quality and the smell of salt dough drying in the oven will fill your kitchen with the aroma of baking bread, and can be very therapeutic.

There are many weird and wonderful recipes for salt dough using different flour and salt ratios, and extra ingredients such as potato flour or cornflour to produce a finer, smoother dough. Adding oil, wallpaper paste and glycerine to make the dough more malleable and easier to knead is sometimes recommended but in my experience, apart for the wallpaper adhesive and occasionally vegetable oil, these extra ingredients are not always necessary and can just add confusion. It is up to you to experiment with different combinations if you feel like it, when you have mastered the art of making the dough. I have found that it is better to stick to one or two recipes that are proven to work. Don't forget that, bar accidents, your salt dough model should last indefinitely. If your aim at the end of this book is to produce models to sell at fairs and through retail outlets, it is essential that you use a tried-and-tested recipe. Salt dough can have an unnerving habit of cracking just when you think that you have done everything to prevent that happening: being an organic substance it is susceptible to changes in the conditions of the environment around it. This is just one of the occupational hazards of working with this medium, and I will explain in the following pages how to minimize this problem.

MAKING SALT DOUGH BY MACHINE

My life was revolutionized when my grandmother lent me her Kenwood Chef food mixer. This sturdy and rather ancient machine with its dough hook attachment churned out pounds and pounds of beautifully smooth dough. This meant that salt dough production at Christmas when all my customers wanted their orders at the same time became far less stressful and I could greet the New Year without the biceps and forearms of a weightlifter!

There is no reason why salt dough cannot be processed in a food mixer, as long as it has a dough hook attachment and a powerful enough motor to cope with seven to ten minutes of kneading. Keep the power setting low to start off with, making sure that the machine kneads rather than beats the dough. If in doubt, follow the manufacturer's instructions and use small quantities. After the machine has worked the dough, turn it out onto a lightly floured surface and pull it together by hand.

Cover and leave to rest for twenty minutes at room temperature.

INGREDIENTS

Flour

There are several theories about suitable flour for salt dough. The choice of flours available these days is so varied that it is sometimes difficult to choose, as each brand boasts of its superior blending properties. I generally go for the middle of the price range – the most expensive is not necessarily the best.

Unbleached plain white flour (or general purpose flour) should always be used if it is available. Quite often, supermarkets' own brands are more suitable than top-of-the-range finely milled flours. Bleached flour produces a tacky dough which makes kneading difficult; it is possible to use this flour, but you will have to work the dough for longer to get it to the correct consistency.

Plain wholemeal (brown flour) is also suitable and makes a nice, nutty-coloured brown dough, but bear in mind that models may take slightly longer to bake.

Self-raising flour is not at all suitable as the raising agent in the flour will distort your model as soon as it goes into the oven.

Strong bread flour has a very high gluten level which gives the dough an elastic texture, making it difficult to model.

Cornflour and potato flour are sometimes used by doughcrafters to produce a fine grade of dough and to make delicate and intricate pieces. By adding a tablespoon of cornflour or potato flour to

the basic dough recipe a much denser dough is produced. I have found the basic dough recipe that I use – which has more salt than traditional recipes – produces the same results.

Salt

Ordinary table salt is the most suitable for dough, and the finer the texture, the better. Some brands of cooking salt can also be used as long as they are not too coarse, or they will produce a gritty-textured dough. It is possible to make salt finer by putting it into a food processor and blending it.

Water

Always use tepid water for mixing the dry ingredients together. This helps dissolve the salt and makes kneading easier. If the water is too hot it has the effect of releasing the gluten in the flour too quickly, and the dough becomes elastic and unmanageable. Some brands of flour absorb more water than others, so it is a good idea to add the water a little at a time until the dough has reached the correct consistency.

Oil

One or two tablespoons of oil can make kneading easier, but are not essential.

Wallpaper Paste/Adhesive

Wallpaper paste acts as a strengthening agent when added to the dough. It is par-

TIP:

If your skin becomes irritated by the salt, use rubber gloves when kneading the dough by hand; it is possible to buy thin surgical gloves to wear whilst modelling. Always wash your hands regularly, and use lots of hand cream.

TIP:

As most adhesives nowadays contain fungicides, care should be taken when cleaning your work surface and tools after using the dough, especially when working in a kitchen where food is prepared. Keep washing your hands during modelling .

ticularly suitable for making flat models and plaques, where the dough is rolled out with a rolling pin to a thickness of 0.5cm (⅛ in). The paste can be added by mixing up a small quantity using the manufacturer's instructions and adding the required amount to the dry ingredients; it will be necessary to adjust the amount of water accordingly.

RECIPES

The following recipes are the ones I have used over and over again, and I have always had good results. I use more salt than the traditional salt dough recipe, which is two of flour and one of salt, and enough water to mix. As I have already mentioned, the more salt in a recipe, the better the modelling potential of the dough; but it is essential to get the balance right. Some recipes use equal quantities of flour and salt, but I have found that this makes the painting stage difficult as the corrosive effect of the salt will shorten the longevity of paints and varnishes. Some acrylic paints also react to a high salt content by becoming patchy when applied to the model.

TIP:

Use either metric or imperial measurements when weighing out the ingredients; do not mix them up, as metric measurements are slightly greater than imperial – using exactly ¼ pint of water with the metric measurement in flour and salt will make your dough too dry.

Basic Dough

This mixture is suitable for all projects where the dough it twisted, rolled, plaited, or used for three-dimensional modelling. It can also be used for making coloured dough.

- 225g (8oz) plain unbleached flour

- 175g (6oz) fine table or cooking salt

- 150ml (¼ pint) tepid water (approx)

Paste Dough

This mixture is suitable for flat models such as plaques, basket bases, mirror frames and large projects that weigh over 250g (10oz). The wallpaper adhesive will give the dough extra strength.

- 225g (8oz) plain unbleached flour

- 175g (6oz) fine table or cooking salt

- 1 tablespoon of made-up wallpaper paste

- Enough tepid water to bind all the ingredients together

Method

Place the dry ingredients in a large bowl and mix together with a spoon; then make a well in the centre and add the water (and paste if required).

Combine all the ingredients until they have formed a ball and the sides of the bowl are clean. If the dough feels too dry, then add a little more water. If the dough feels too wet, then add a little more flour. Turn the dough out onto a lightly floured work surface about 2ft (60cm) square. Kitchen worktops such as formica or smooth wood are fine for kneading, though a marble slab or cool tiled worktop provides the ideal base.

You may find the dough easier to knead if you divide it into two batches; if you do this, cover one batch so that it does not dry out and put it to one side. Start to knead the dough by pushing it down hard with a forward movement, using the heel of one hand. Repeat this several times and keep turning the dough with your other hand to ensure even pressure. Keep repeating the process for at least ten minutes – this is a good opportunity to get rid of some of the day's tension and stress! The dough will start to feel smooth, pliable and slightly warm to the touch; this is when you know that you are reaching the correct texture and consistency.

To test that the dough is ready for modelling, roll a sausage of dough and hold it up: it should keep its shape.

Finally, wrap the dough in a plastic bag and leave at room temperature to rest for at least twenty minutes to allow the gluten in the dough to settle.

COLOURING DOUGH BEFORE BAKING

Colouring dough before baking is a matter of preference and convenience, as there is a definite advantage in using coloured dough for projects that have a lot of detail with small fiddly pieces that overlap and make painting difficult such as leaves, strawberries, holly berries, cherries and blue, red or yellow flowers. For projects that use dark colours such as black and brown hair and dark clothing on figures, and manes and tails on ponies, using coloured dough is easier and any subtle colour changes during the baking stage don't really show. Making up batches of colours that you use a lot is a more convenient way of working, especially if you are making large quantities of dough. Freeze the different coloured dough in small blocks wrapped in plastic for future use.

Natural products can also be used, such as powdered instant coffee, cocoa, paprika, curry powder, turmeric and beetroot juice, although I cannot recommend the smell! Some food colouring dyes can be used, although not all colours are suitable and they have a tendency to fade over a period of time. I tend to use green for leaves and grass, the other colour ranges available not being as versatile as artists' colours.

Experiment first with food colour by mixing a small amount into a ball of ready-made dough and work it in until it has blended to the required shade. The main disadvantage of using coloured dough is that the baking process changes the hue of a lot of colours, so bear in mind that the end result may not be the colour you started with. White and pastel colours do not bake well and are better left, if it is convenient, to air-dry somewhere warm. I find it easier to paint on light colours afterwards, using water colours.

To make up small amounts of coloured dough, follow the method below; for larger quantities use the basic dough recipe:

Measure out two heaped tablespoons of flour and one of salt, and mix together in the bowl.

Add approximately half a teaspoon of poster paint or water colour, or one teaspoon of food colour, and enough water

TIP:

The reason for the long kneading stage is to ensure that there is no air left in the dough, which can lead to cracking later on. It is almost impossible to overknead the dough by hand; in fact, the more it is handled, the better.

to combine the mixture together. Wearing rubber gloves, knead until smooth.

STORAGE OF RAW DOUGH

Excess dough can be kept for one day, wrapped in a plastic bag at room temperature. After this time it will darken, go soft and become difficult to model. Storing the dough in a fridge will give it an elastic texture and make modelling almost impossible. Freezing, on the other hand, does it no harm and any plain or coloured dough left over from a project can be frozen successfully and kept indefinitely for future use.

When the dough is required again, defrost for a couple of hours, add a little warm water and knead until smooth. This is a good way of planning ahead and making sure that you always have ready-made dough available, especially if you are making large quantities and using a lot different colours.

PROBLEM SOLVING BEFORE BAKING/DRYING

The Dough Feels Sticky:

This can be caused by bleached flours; persevere and keep kneading, dusting the dough lightly with flour as you work.

The Dough Feels Gritty:

The salt is too coarse; try using a finer grade of salt or, if all else fails, start again and grind the salt first in a food processor.

The Dough is Crumbling and Cracking During Modelling:

The dough is too dry; add a little water with your hands and knead until smooth.

The Dough is Too Soft and will not Hold its Shape:

There is too much water in the dough; add some flour and keep kneading until the texture becomes firm.

Sausages of Dough Split When Being Rolled:

Insufficient kneading causes air bubbles which will make rolling thin ropes or sausages of dough difficult: they will split lengthways and look uneven and lumpy. Gather the dough up into a ball, and knead again with lightly floured hands.

3 Modelling

The malleable nature of the dough lends itself to certain types of modelling, such as plaiting, twisting, rolling , bas relief, three-dimensional models, and sculptured and flat plaques. There are no hard-and-fast rules about the size of your model, although some practical considerations should be taken into account. As salt dough is very brittle it is more suited to making decorative pieces for hanging on walls, and care must be taken with three-dimensional and free standing models. The size of the model is also determined by the height and width of your oven, and how you are going to display it – a dough ring weighing more than 1kg (2lb) may have problems staying on its hanging loop if it gets damp.

For your first salt dough project, choose something small and easily assembled like a card decorated with dough cut-outs or a simple twisted dough ring decorated with some flowers and leaves. If you do not get your shape right at first, don't worry; push it all together and start again. As you become more proficient, try your hand at, say, a mirror frame project, a candlestick holder or a pencil cup. Treat the dough just like modelling clay and make a gnome for your kitchen or some fruit to fill a bowl or basket.

There are many projects that can be adapted to make gifts for special occasions: for Mother's Day, try your hand at making a bunch of dough roses using a combination of coloured and painted dough; for Valentine's Day, make a heart-shaped mirror frame. As those cold winter evenings draw in and you are constantly being reminded that Christmas is just around the corner, salt dough comes into its own. The variety of decorations and gifts that can be made by the whole family for very little expense is immense, and if you are planning to sell at craft fairs and Christmas bazaars, it is a good idea to start building up your stock well in advance.

BASIC TECHNIQUES

Making a Rope or Sausage of Dough

Use this technique as a base for rings, wreaths and plaits. Take a small ball of well-kneaded dough in your hand and gently pull it out into a sausage shape on a lightly floured surface. Starting in the middle, gently roll to and fro using the fingers of both hands and spreading them as you go along, exerting even pressure until you have the desired length and thickness.

Making a Twist of Dough

This technique is used as the base for most wreaths, handles and decorative trim for basket plaques, edging around name plaques, frames, candle holders and rims for dough bowls. Take two sausages of dough of equal length, lay the top one diagonally across the centre of the bottom one and twist together, starting from the middle and working outwards. By starting in the middle, the twist will be even and not become stretched. When you have finished one

1. Always make sure that the dough is well kneaded and pliable.

2. Do not over-wet models when assembling.

3 . Always work on a piece of parchment for ease of movement.

4 . Keep any spare dough covered while you are working.

5. If your model needs a hanging loop, insert it before baking.

6. Bake as soon as possible after modelling, unless air drying.

7. Wash and dry all metal tools, otherwise they will go rusty.

side, start on the other and tidy the ends with a knife before joining.

Plaiting

With a little practice, you can take the basic sausage rolling technique and use it to make plaits or braids of different widths and lengths. It is very important that the dough is the correct consistency, and a slightly firm dough is easier to work with, otherwise you will have problems with stretching. Take three sausages of dough of equal length and width and join them together at one end with a dab of water. Then fan the three pieces of dough out so that they do not get tangled as you work, and start to plait just like braiding hair, making sure that they are even all the way. Tidy the ends off with a knife and lift gently on to

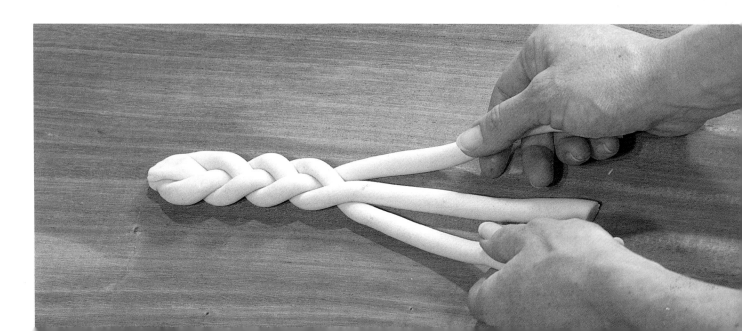

some parchment before making it into your chosen shape. This technique can be used to make mirror frames, basket bases for wall plaques, wreaths and decorative table centres for holding candles.

Rolling, Flat Plaques and Templates

The dough is rolled out flat with a rolling pin; if possible, use one with a revolving barrel which will distribute the pressure evenly on the dough. This technique forms the basis for making flat wall plaques, bowls and frames, and for using templates and cutters. Use the paste recipe for larger pieces like free-standing bowls and frames, and basic dough for smaller cut-outs and when using templates. If the dough has been kneaded correctly it should be so pliable that it can be rolled very thinly and used to make flowers, leaves, ribbons and items of clothing for figures. You can drape and fold layers of thin dough over figures, creating the effect of movement and making them more three-dimensional.

ADVANCED TECHNIQUES

Three-Dimensional Models

Three-dimensional modelling and sculpturing will require some free style and creative input. Most of the models are assembled using rolls of dough attached to each other using water; models over 8cm (3in) tall will need supporting with cocktail sticks or wire, as the dough will spread a little in the oven and the model will loose its shape. An eye for dimension is needed and although I have described in the projects that follow how to assemble figures, you can create your own style by adding different characteristics and facial expressions. The size and density of the model will determine the length of baking time. Larger pieces can be assembled over a ball of foil and this will help reduce the baking time by half. Another way to reduce the baking time of a large, dense model is to actually hollow it out after the first hour, using a teaspoon to scoop out the soft dough, leaving a crust of dough of about 1cm (½in) thick, and then returning it to the oven to finish baking.

Free-Standing Models Using a Mould

Using an ovenproof bowl or dish to act as a support mould to make bowls out of dough is a very simple way of achieving a stunning effect and making something that is serviceable. Glass bottles and jam jars can be used as moulds to make vases

or pots from dough. Always choose bowls without a rim and bottles and jars with straight sides, otherwise you will have trouble getting the dough past the rim once it has hardened. As long as the oven is kept at a steady 100°C the glass is quite safe, and as it heats up it con-

ducts the heat through the dough, speeding up the baking time. You can use a microwave with this technique, especially if you are planning to paint the model afterwards. Another handy tool I discovered in my local cook shop is a plastic lattice piecrust cutter which, with just a quick flick of a rolling pin, turns sheets of thin dough into excellent bases for bowls with neat diagonal holes. The dough is prevented from sticking by wrapping the mould in parchment or cling film. Small pieces can be eased off the mould after about one hour's baking and then returned to the oven to finish off. Larger pieces will need the support of the mould and should be left until hard, and after baking allowed to cool first before gently lifting the dough off the mould.

If the bowls are to be used for bread, biscuits or sweets, leave them unvarnished and just store the dough bowl at room temperature when not in use.

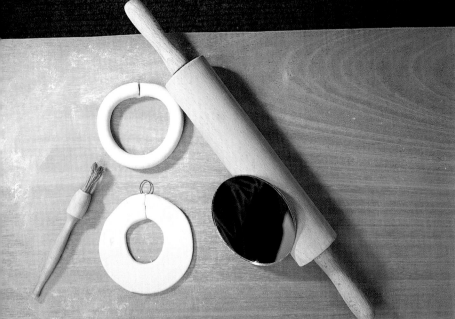

Mirror Frames

The dough lends itself very well to making frames, by either the twisting, plaiting or rolling methods. As I have mentioned before, always use paste dough for added strength. In the interests of safety I would not recommend making large picture frames or mirror frames to hang on walls, because of the risk of the frame cracking if it ever got damp. An A5-size frame should support the weight of a mirror if it is to be hung on a wall, and smaller frames with a backing support made from card are ideal for standing on a desk or sideboard. The frames can be painted using specialist finishing techniques like bronzing and verdigris, or by creating an antiquing effect with crackle glaze. Small frames for children's bedrooms can be decorated with animal cut-outs or

flowers painted in bright primary colours.

Mirrors can be bought at your local building suppliers where they can be cut to any size or shape. Most D.I.Y stores sell mirror tiles which you can use if it is more convenient. Mirror frames are easy to assemble: the unbaked dough frame can be put directly onto the mirror edge after damping it slightly first, then place the whole thing on a lined baking tray and put it in the oven at 100°C until it is baked. The heat of the mirror will make the dough bond onto it like glue. Always allow the mirror frame to cool slowly in the oven so that it doesn't crack. To fin-ish the mirror decorate and varnish it carefully, masking the glass with paper to avoid getting varnish on it. You can back the mirror with a piece of felt or a cork tile for a neater finish

MODELLING FRUIT AND FLOWERS

Modelling fruit out of salt dough can be very rewarding as it is possible to make the fruit very realistic. You will have to use some free style modelling skills to make three-dimensional fruit. This fruit

can be used to fill a wicker basket or bowl and can look very effective, especially when care is taken with the painting to make it as life-like as possible, and makes a refreshing change from the plastic fruit arrangements often seen in gift shops. Fruit-filled baskets, wall plaques, wreaths, plaits, dough bowls, figures holding baskets of fruit – all these projects sell very well at craft fairs and in craft shops. Fill your oven with dough fruit that are all roughly the same size and density so that they bake evenly. Cherries and strawberries will take less time, and can be baked in a couple of hours.

The secret in painting the fruit is in keeping the colours as subtle and true to the original as possible. Using water colours and gouache paints, the natural colour of the dough comes through giving the fruit a mellow hue. You can also experiment with different varnishes, using a gloss for cherries, strawberries and apples, a satin for oranges, pears, bananas and grapes, and a matt acrylic varnish for peaches, apricots and plums.

Vegetables, like fruit, need the modelling skills of nimble fingers as there are not many carrot- or cabbage-shaped cutters available! Have a life-sized example of the vegetable you are trying to copy in front of you and use it as a guide.

It is easy to cheat when making flowers as there are so many cutters now available that the days when I would painstakingly make individual petals for daisies and primroses are over. Roses, however, still take a little time, but once you have got the hang of it you will find that a simple roll of dough made into the shape of a rose will look very realistic. Once you have made your flower shapes the painting and finishing off can really improve the look of a project, especially when it is dominated by one or two colours, as in a basket of strawberries: small blossoms painted white will add contrast and high-

light the red of the fruit. I have found that people love flowers and many of my models with flower themes have found their way to new homes.

Apples

Take a ball of well-kneaded basic dough and roll it gently in the palm of your hand until smooth and round. Press a clove into the base of the apple to make a calyx; then make an indentation in the top of the apple with a skewer or the pointed end of a paintbrush and press the stem of a clove into it to make a stalk. For an extra touch, add a couple of small leaves around the base of the stalk. Give the apple an undercoat of yellow water colour; when that has dried, dab on some red scarlet with a sponge, leave it to dry and paint some very fine streaks of crimson. Add some pale green around the calyx.

Bananas

Roll out two or more small sausages of dough and gently form into a banana shape; mark a line on each banana with the back of the knife. Add slightly shorter sausages of dough on top to create the effect of a bunch. Bananas as a rule look better in an arrangement of fruit where they can blend in. Three-dimensional bananas take a bit of practice to ensure that they do not look too flat. Paint your bananas using a creamy yellow and add a few brown spots to make them look more realistic

Cherries

This is a job you can do in front of the TV, especially if you are making a lot of them. It is a good idea to make up a batch of red dough; the best red colours I have found are alzarian red gouache by Windsor & Newton and a crimson water colour or gouache by Daler Rowney. It is important to use a darkish red for colouring the dough, otherwise the result may be a bright pink. You can give the cherries an added lick of crimson paint when they have been baked. To make the fruit, simply roll small balls of dough with your fingers; I like to make my cherries in pairs, as it makes them easier to paint and varnish afterwards. The stalks are made with black cotton stamens which are used by sugar crafters when making flowers out of icing sugar paste. They are available in most sugar-craft shops; alternatively, you can use real dried cherry stalks, which look very realistic, though they can get very brittle when baked so have to be treated with care. After the cherries are baked, varnish them by dipping them into the tin, holding the cherries by their stalks, and threading them onto a long piece of stick balanced on two jam jars over some newspaper to drain.

Grapes

As with the cherries, it is sometimes easier to make up some purple or green dough. Using the same rolling technique as above, make lots of small balls of dough and arrange them into the shape of a bunch of grapes using water to stick the balls together. Add a small twig and a leaf at the top of the bunch for effect. For a seasonal Christmas feel you can spray bunches of grapes with gold or silver spray before varnishing.

Lemons

Take a ball of dough and roll it in your hands until smooth; then pull either end

out slightly to make the lemon shape, and gently roll it backwards and forwards over the fine gauge of a cheese grater to create the pitted effect on the lemon's skin. When baked, paint with a watery lemon yellow wash and add a touch of light green at either end.

Peaches and Apricots

Take a ball of dough and roll and model in your hands into the shape of a peach. With the back of the knife, gently press a line from the top of the peach halfway down towards the base. Using the pointed end of a fine paintbrush, make an indentation and push in the stem of a clove or a piece of twig so that it is just showing, to make the peach stem. Apricots can be made in the same way, making them smaller than the peaches. Choose subtle creamy pinks with a slight orange tint when painting peaches and apricots. When they have dried, dip a small sponge in some flame-red water colour and gently add a reddish bloom to the fruit. These fruit look better in a subdued varnish like a satin or even matt finish, as they do not need the high shine of an apple.

Plums

Make as above, but the shape of your plum should be more oval and you should give the plum a small stalk. Paint in a mixture of purple water colour with a little red.

Oranges

As with the lemons, take a ball of dough and roll and mould it using your hands; imagine the shape of a real orange or, even better, have one in front of you that

you can copy. Roll the ball of dough across the fine gauge of a cheese grater until all the sides have a pitted texture. Using a small, sharp knife, make a criss-cross in the middle of the orange and press in the top of a clove to make the calyx. Use a slightly smaller ball of dough to make satsumas and mandarins. Paint the oranges with yellow water colour mixed with a little scarlet to make a watery orange. When they are dry, emphasize the calyx on the orange with black water colour.

Pears

Take a ball of dough and work it in your hands, gently pulling one end until it forms a pear shape. Use the back of the knife to gently press a line halfway down the pear to the base to make a shallow groove like a William's pear, or leave it round like a Conference pear. Press the starshape of the clove into the base of the pear and the stem of the clove to make the pear stalk. If you have got more than one pear in the arrangement, paint one of them in a sap green water colour and another in a creamy light yellow with a touch of leaf green. Add little freckles on the yellow pear with a very fine paintbrush dipped in brown sienna.

Raspberries/Blackberries

These can be quite painstaking to make and look much better as part of an arrangement of fruit, in either a wreath or a basket plaque. Each individual berry is assembled by rolling tiny balls of dough with your fingers and moulding them together into the shape of the fruit with a damp brush. Alternatively, using a piece of fabric netting or even a wire sieve, push a small piece of dough

through the holes, lift off gently with a knife and place directly on to the model. Paint the raspberries in a dark alzarian crimson and the blackberries in purple mixed with a touch of black.

Strawberries

If you are making a lot of strawberries for an arrangement, model them in different sizes and use red dough for the fruit and green for the leaves and hulls. Roll small balls of dough in your hands, pulling one end gently into a slight point. Roll out a piece of dough thinly and, using a blossom cutter, press out some shapes to make strawberry hulls and join them on to the fruit using a damp brush. Give the strawberries their pitted appearance by making small dents in the dough using a cocktail stick or skewer. Alternatively, paint the baked fruit with a watery wash of scarlet water colour, and the hulls a sap green.

HANGING FINISHED MODELS

There are various methods of hanging models, the most efficient being thin horticultural training wire, which is available at most garden centres. The wire comes in various different gauges, the thinnest being the best. The plastic coating protects the wire from the eventual corrosive effects of the salt and the heat of the oven up to 150°C, gas mark 1½, will not damage it. You will need a small pair of pliers to cut the wire with. You can make hanging loops of any size by cutting the required length, bending it into a loop and twisting the wire ends together three or four times; splay the two wire ends apart and bend them upwards to give extra holding power to

TIP:

It is not advisable to mix salt dough fruit together with real fruit in a bowl or basket, because after a while the salt in the dough fruit will attract the moisture in the real fruit and the dough fruit will go soft.

rings and wreaths. Paperclips can also be used, and are ideal for smaller pieces: they do not bend very easily and it is sometimes necessary to thread a piece of ribbon through them. Hairpins should be bent upwards to give extra hold in the dough. Small holes can be made in the dough by using a drinking straw; this will make a neat hole that will not close up during baking, and a thin piece of ribbon or string can be used to make a hanging loop.

4 Baking and Drying

There seems to be quite a lot of confusion about the baking or drying process of the dough. Some doughcraft artists never put their models in an oven and just rely on air dying, whilst others bake theirs at varying temperatures and times, sometimes leaving the oven door ajar to let the air circulate, and others even bake them with the Sunday joint!

The wonderful thing about salt dough is that you can leave it somewhere warm to dry, or bake it in a conventional oven or, in some cases, even a microwave. The dough is dried out very slowly like a meringue, rather than baked like bread. The golden rule when drying the dough is that *the lower the temperature and the longer the drying time, the better.* Most dough models will bake happily at approximately 100°C, gas mark ½. Generally, flat models will start to blister and warp at higher temperatures, while thicker twisted and plaited wreaths and rings can stand a temperature of 150°C, gas mark 1½. Once the model is baked hard, any gradual rise in temperature will not harm it. As all ovens vary according to their age and condition you can not always rely on the oven settings, and it is a good idea to invest in an oven thermometer.

If the thought of putting something in the oven for up to eight hours or even more sounds very extravagant and not at all energy saving, bear in mind that you are using a very low setting. To start off with, make a small model that will only take two or three hours, and as you become more proficient you will learn to bake more than one model at a time and economize by making sure that your oven is full to capacity! There are various ways to reduce the baking times by putting the model straight onto the oven shelf after the first couple of hours, or turning it and moving it up onto the top shelf.

As you become more confident, you can experiment with oven baking times and temperatures and learn how to achieve different finishes by turning the temperature up a few degrees; however, to start off with use the recommended baking times for each of the projects.

Plastic-coated training wire used to make hanging loops and small cones, dried flowers, seeds and pieces of mirror will withstand 100°C and not come to any harm. I have even put wicker baskets filled with dough fruit to dry out overnight in my oven with brilliant results and no harm done to either basket or fruit. Obviously, if you wish to bake a project at a higher temperature then you will have to take into account that the plastic on the hanging loop may melt and any dried flower or cones will become very brittle.

TYPES OF OVEN

Gas and Electric Ovens

As mentioned above, use the lowest setting and always allow the finished models to cool in the oven before taking them out as this helps to prevent cracking. It is quite safe to open the oven door whilst they are drying, and the temperature can be turned up 10–20°C towards the end of baking to speed things along and to add a golden brown finish to the models.

Fan-Assisted Ovens

These ovens tend to be hotter than conventional gas and electric ovens; if in doubt, check with an oven thermometer.

Agas/Rayburns

If you are lucky enough to own an Aga or a Rayburn then this is the ideal oven for salt dough because you can just put it in the warming oven and forget about it. Always check the temperature first, though, and when the models are finished take them out and leave near the top so they cool down slowly.

Microwave Ovens

These will undoubtedly speed up the drying process, and are most suited to small models and dough cut-outs that can be dried in ten to twenty minutes. As with conventional cookers, microwaves vary greatly so it is best to experiment first with some flat dough to get the drying times right. It is often necessary to dry the dough in stages of ten minutes plus ten minutes and then five minutes plus five minutes, and so on. The disadvantage is that the dough takes on a pale, insipid appearance and bubbles can form on flat surfaces. Models have a tendency to crack more easily than drying the conventional way. I would not recommend that any models intended for sale are dried in a microwave as there is no guarantee that cracks will not form later on.

Air Drying

This is the most economical way to dry models, although not very practical as it can take a couple of weeks to dry out a model 1cm (½in) thick. However, it is an ideal way to dry small, thin models that children have made and is quite often used in primary schools. The models are left uncovered in a warm place like an airing cupboard or boiler room, or placed on a wire tray over a radiator. If it is summer and hot, then they can be left in the sun to dry out. The models need to be turned regularly so that they dry evenly and are usually improved with a coat of brightly coloured paint which will enhance the finished result.

PREPARING THE DOUGH FOR BAKING

When your model is ready to be baked, transfer onto an ungreased, lined, flat baking tray. Rounded shapes such as rings, wreaths, plaits, dough dollies' faces and arms, and fruit can be brushed over lightly with a little water using a pastry brush. This has the effect of plumping the dough out and getting rid of any uneven marks and creases on the dough. In contrast this should not be done to flat pieces of dough such as baskets and plaques, in fact any piece of dough that has been rolled out with a rolling pin. The water encourages the dough to blister and dry unevenly; again this is something that you will master with practice.

THE BAKING PROCESS

Place the baking tray in a pre-heated oven on the middle shelf for the first hour. The model will start to form a thin white crust and become set into its shape. Once this has happened it is quite safe to move it up to the top shelf where it will bake slightly quicker without warping or losing its shape, unless

the oven is turned up suddenly to a very high temperature. Once the model is semi-hard you can take it off the baking tray and, keeping it on a piece of baking parchment, put it directly onto the oven shelf: this helps to speed up the baking time by allowing the heat to get directly underneath the model. At the end of the allocated baking time check that the model is dried right through by picking it up using oven gloves and tapping the underside: it should feel hard and sound hollow. Then turn the oven off and leave to cool down slowly.

GLAZES

The colour of the dough can be altered in the oven to a golden brown finish like newly baked bread or biscuits by applying different glazes. This method gives the dough a rustic, natural look, especially for projects like wheat sheaves, fruit wreaths and salt dough bread. The glazes should be applied during the last hour of baking and only on the parts that are not going to be painted over later. Sometimes paints and varnishes do not adhere very well on to glazed dough.

TIP:

It is possible to re-bake models by placing them in a cold oven and warming them through slowly. This is a convenient way to finish off models that have been air-dried or part baked in the microwave.

Egg Glaze

For a deep brown and shiny finish use one egg beaten with one tablespoon of water.

Brush on to the model and turn the oven up ten degrees. Watch it carefully as it will go brown very quickly.

Soy Glaze

This will give a uniform satin brown finish. Use two tablespoons of dark soy mixed with one of water, and brush on every twenty minutes. This glaze does not burn at high temperatures.

Salt Water Glaze

This is by far the simplest and is just a matter of brushing the model over with water every twenty minutes after turning the oven up ten degrees during the final hour of baking. It gives the dough a biscuit colour which is highlighted when varnished.

PROBLEM-SOLVING DURING AND AFTER BAKING

Blistering

This usually happens to flat models and can be caused by higher oven temperatures, or insufficient kneading causing air bubbles in the dough which will start to expand as soon as the dough heats up. Excess water on flat models will heat up faster than the dough and can cause blistering. If the oven temperature is over 100°C, then reduce it and gently prick the blister with a pin while it is still soft and press any air out with your fingers.

Cracks Appear in Plaited and Twisted Dough

This often happens when the dough has not been kneaded properly and trapped air causes dents and creases in the dough. Unfortunately, these cracks tend appear towards the end of the baking time when it is too late to start again. There is not much you can do to rectify this other than make up a little paste of dough mixed with water to fill the cracks and return it to the oven to harden off. When the model has finished baking, sand off any rough edges where the cracks have been filled and if necessary paint over them so that they blend in.

Under-Cooking

The model will look pale and slightly grey in colour and feel heavy. Check the oven temperature as it may be too cool; turn it up to 120°C and move the model to the top shelf and leave until baked hard.

Over-Cooking

It is virtually impossible to over-cook salt dough, some larger models can be left in the bottom of an Aga or Rayburn for days, although I do not recommend this in a conventional oven because of the high fuel consumption. However, it is quite easy to burn your model if the oven is turned up suddenly, especially when browning off using an egg glaze. There is also the danger of uneven cooking temperature causing cracks to appear later on.

Model Cracks After it has been Baked

This is generally caused by a sudden change in temperature. Allow the models to cool slowly in the oven after baking whenever possible. Cracks on the underside of the model are all right and can be filled with varnish and sealed. Small cracks on the front of the model can be repaired with strong general purpose adhesive and filled with Polyfilla or wood filler. You may have to paint over the cracks later to cover them. Try to paint and varnish your model as soon as possible after baking. If this is not convenient, then store it somewhere warm like an airing cupboard until you are ready to decorate it.

TIP:

Always leave salt dough models to cool in the oven after baking: this helps prevent cracks from forming due to a sudden change in temperature.

5 Paints and Varnishes

Once your salt dough model is baked/dried, it is ready to be decorated. This is your opportunity to create your own style in the choice of colour schemes and painting techniques. I will guide you with a choice of colours and paints suitable for the projects that follow. Great fun can be had by experimenting with different finishing techniques: you can choose either to enhance the look of the dough by using colours that bring out the mellow golden browns of the natural dough, or to completely change the look to simulate wood, metal, fabric, ceramic or clay. Look around your kitchen at everyday household objects like old china plates, bowls and cups with interesting patterns. Art books, interior design books, magazines and fabric swatches with modern, contemporary designs can all provide you with ideas and inspiration.

There are many different colours, paint types and finishing methods that can be used in painting the dough. The most economical are poster colours and water colours found in children's paint boxes; although these are fine for simple projects, you will need to invest in a set of good quality artists' colours if you want to create a more professional finish and sell your work. A mixture of designers' gouache, water colours and some water-based acrylics in the primary colours provide a good foundation from which to work with. All these paints are compatible with the high salt content in the dough and with the varnish used to seal it with. It is also advisable to have some good quality paintbrushes, as these are your tools for painting and the better the quality of brush, the easier it is

to be precise and accurate in your painting technique. You will need a couple of fine brushes that make a good point for detailed work, some medium brushes with good springy flexible tips for getting into tight corners and a couple of broader brushes for painting larger areas. Unfortunately, the rough surface of the dough does wear brushes out, so I use a mixture of nylon, hog bristle and dalon, which is a durable man-made synthetic sable.

THE PAINTS

The following paints are ones that I have used successfully over the years and have withstood the corrosive effects of the salt.

Acrylic Water-Based Paint

These paints are available in a full range of colours including, gold, silver and bronze. They come in tubes and pots of differing sizes depending on the make. They are water-based and brushes are easily washed after use. A word of warning, however: they dry incredibly quickly, so any mistakes must be mopped up right away and brushes always washed off as soon as you have finished with them. I use permanent white as a base to mix with other water colours to make pastels. This paint provides a good smooth matt base which seals the surface of the dough, making it ideal for painting patterns on. Some dark acrylics can go patchy on the dough: this is because they have differ-

ent pigment strengths. This problem can be rectified by mixing a small amount of the same colour of water colour or gouache into the acrylic and then applying it to the dough. Acrylics can also be painted on to the model after it has been varnished, which is useful if you need to retouch the paint after repairing breakages or cracks.

Designers' Gouache

These paints have a very rich, strong colour and a little will go a long way. They are available in a wide range of colours and mix well with acrylics. Most colours are graded to show their permanence with star ratings: three stars means that the colours will not fade if kept under normal conditions, and these I have found are most suitable for salt dough. However, care should be taken when applying the paint not to overload the brush, as the paint may craze as it dries.

Water Colour

Available in tubes and palettes, these paints can be diluted and used to add a wash of translucent colour over the dough. Any mistakes can easily be corrected by using a damp cotton wool bud or a piece of kitchen roll. They can also be used to colour the dough before baking.

Poster Colour

These come in handy pots and are ideal for children to use. They are easily mixed with water, and brushes and surfaces are easily cleaned up afterwards. They can also be used to colour the dough before baking.

Hobby/Craft Paints

These are available from hobby/art shops and come in small pots of brightly coloured acrylic-type paint. Ideal for covering large areas of dough, the result is a solid matt finish.

Specialist Paint Finishes

There are many paint finishing products on the market that you can use to create a different finish on the dough. Crackle glaze can be applied to frames and flat plaques to give an antique look. Bronzing and gilt can be used and some manufacturers will supply kits of paint to achieve such a result. Enamel and spray paints are also suitable and can be applied to the dough on top of the varnish.

THE PAINTING PROCESS

Preparing Your Work Place

You will need, apart from your paints and brushes, the following: a flat palette or plate for mixing the paints; two water pots, one for light colours and one for dark; and a roll of kitchen paper and some cotton wool buds for mopping up mistakes and drying your brushes with. Work on old newspapers and make sure that you have a good source of light: it often surprises me how colours can look very different in natural light. I always check the colour of a model before I have finished by taking it outside and looking at it in daylight – quite often the project can look too bright and needs toning down a little. You must take into account when you are painting your project that the varnish will darken most colours, and depending on the type of varnish may also turn light colours slightly yellow (see 'Varnishing').

Painting the Dough

Prepare the dough model for painting by sanding off rough edges and brushing off any loose flour or salt. Having chosen your colours, apply the paint using even strokes, taking care not to over-wet the dough, and dab any excess water away with a piece of kitchen roll. Gouache paints and water colours need to be applied thinly and can then be washed over with a brush dipped in water to blend the colours in. If you do not like the effect and want to start again, then gently wipe the paint off with damp tissue, let it dry and start again. A small piece of synthetic sponge dipped in some paint is ideal for dabbing red onto apples and other fruit. Use it to add a bronzed or gilded finish to bowls and frames. Leave the painted model for an hour or so to thoroughly dry before varnishing.

VARNISHING THE MODEL

This is an essential stage of doughcrafting, for varnish preserves the life of your salt dough model. Without varnish the salt in the dough will draw in moisture from the atmosphere – it may be from a steaming kettle in a small kitchen, hanging by an open window or in a bathroom. Damp houses with no central heating are not suitable for salt dough. Wet, humid summers are a doughcrafter's worst nightmare, as even the most carefully varnished pieces can go soft and drop off the wall. I had the embarrassing experience once of having to apologize on behalf of a salt dough ring I had made for a customer that had fallen off the wall and demolished the lady's antique china heirloom. The ring was perfectly all right and just needed a new hanging loop.

Like the vast array of paints available, there are as many varnishes on the market. It can be quite daunting to go into a DIY store and stand in front of a shelf with wood varnishes that seems to stretch the whole length of the aisle. The choice of varnishes with different woodstains, sizes and finishes is immense, but all you need is small tin of spirit-based clear polyurethane interior wood varnish, either satin or gloss, a soft var-

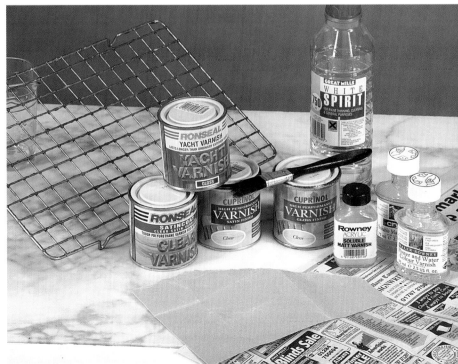

nishing brush and some white spirit. For free-standing models such as bowls or candle holders you can use yacht varnish. This is very hard wearing and will give your model a high gloss shine. The brand of the varnish does not matter as they all have the same properties, but you should avoid acrylic water-based wood varnish, as it dries leaving an opaque film over the dough.

If you want to preserve the light colours on your model, then you can use specialist poster and water colour and matt acrylic varnishes. These are available from art shops and are used to preserve water colour and oil paintings. Although they do not have the durability of wood varnish, they can be used in conjunction with it by varnishing the main body and the back of the model with the more durable wood varnish, then changing brushes and highlighting any light colours such as flowers, light pieces of clothing and ribbons with the water colour varnish. The matt acrylic varnish has a non-bloom finish; it is entirely up to you which one you choose.

The Varnishing Process

Make sure that the surface is thoroughly dry. Use a small amount of varnish on the tip of your brush and, gently starting with the back of your model, work the varnish into the surface, filling any small cracks and joins.

Lay the model on newspaper to dry and then repeat the process on the front. To speed this up, use an old wire cake cooling rack to dry the models on; this means that you can varnish back and front at the same time. I recommend that you apply three coats of varnish, making sure that each coat is dry before the next application. Most varnishes take two to four hours to dry between coats.

TIP:

When varnishing a lot of models, use thin, disposable plastic gloves to protect your hands.

PROBLEM SOLVING DURING PAINTING AND VARNISHING

Colours Craze

This sometimes happens with some gouache paints when applied too thickly. Use a little acrylic and mix the two paints together for a smoother finish.

Light Colours Go Yellow

This is caused by the polyurethane wood varnish yellowing over a period of time, usually about a year. It is really a matter of personal preference, but not essential, to use matt acrylic or water colour varnish to preserve those lighter colours.

Dark Patches Appear in the Natural, Unpainted Dough

This is caused by tiny cracks that have formed on the surface of the dough and the varnish bleeding into them causing dark, oily patches. Again, try not to let the baked models sit around for too long. Do not saturate the model with varnish as the dough will absorb it rather like a sponge. These patches will eventually disappear as the varnish dries out.

Varnish Becomes Flaky and Cracks After Time

The model has got wet either through condensation or steam. If it can be repaired, sand off the old varnish where possible, repair the paintwork and re-varnish.

Small White Spots Forming on Unpainted Varnished Dough

This is the salt eating its way through the varnish, and generally happens after a couple of years. Lightly sand the surface of the model with fine sandpaper and re-varnish.

Model Cracks After Several Weeks

This can happen to flat models and is caused by insufficient baking time and the fact that the outside edges dry faster than the centre of the plaque. If the crack is at the back of the model, then fill with a woodfiller and re-varnish. If it is in the front and can be filled without spoiling the look of it, then this is the best remedy, otherwise make another one!

Models Fall Off the Wall Once Hung

The model has got damp. High humidity during the summer and heavy rainfall can often make salt dough soft. Place the model in an airing cupboard for a few days until it has gone hard.

AFTERCARE OF MODELS

Although salt dough will last indefinitely, it does need re-varnishing after a couple of years. Avoid hanging your model over a radiator and keep it at room temperature wherever possible. During humid, damp summers it may be necessary to move it to an airing cupboard to prevent it going soft. Do not be tempted to give your model a bath or a quick wash with the dishes! Gently wipe it over with a damp cloth and dry carefully using a hairdryer to get into those nooks and crannies. Although it may be tempting to hang a Christmas wreath made of salt dough on your front door, it is not weather- or rain-proof and you may find a soggy mess on your doorstep in the morning.

The Projects

The designs featured in the following pages are intended to guide and inspire you to create something in your own style. The projects cover all the techniques already described and the illustrations are there for reference. I have set out some general tips to help you:

All projects use the basic dough or paste recipe in the quantities described in 'Making the Dough' and are modelled on to parchment.

Specific tools necessary will be listed for each project.

All the models will need to be baked on a flat baking tray at approximately 100–120°C, gas mark ½, unless stated otherwise. If possible, always check the oven temperature with a gauge.

All the models are varnished with a polyurethane clear wood varnish unless stated otherwise.

Holly Ring

These small holly rings are a good project to get started with as they use the simple twisting technique. Holly leaf cutters are available in most cook shops or you can use the tip of a sharp knife. You can either colour the dough for the leaves and berries using food colour or poster colour before baking, or paint them with water colours afterwards. Decorate the ring with a wire-edged ribbon made into a bow, or make some Christmas roses using the blossom cutters. This quantity of dough will make two rings 15cm (6in) in diameter.

You will need

FOR MODELLING

- One batch of basic dough
- Flour for dusting
- Soy glaze
- Small, sharp knife
- Rolling pin
- Holly leaf cutter
- Set of three blossom cutters
- Water brush
- Baking parchment
- Flat baking tray
- Hanging loop

FOR PAINTING AND VARNISHING

- Artists' paintbrushes
- Dark green and crimson water colours
- White and yellow acrylic
- Clear wood varnish
- Decorative ribbon (optional)
- General purpose glue

Method

Roll out two sausages of dough 26cm (10in) long and the thickness of a finger. Twist them together to form an even coil of dough (see diagram techniques), arrange in a circle on some parchment, remove any excess dough with the knife, damp the ends and insert the hanging loop.

Roll out some thin dough, press out six holly leaf shapes and arrange them on the ring. Add some small balls of dough for berries and some Christmas roses (see 'Flowers') to either the top of the ring, covering the hanging hook, or on the base of the ring, later adding the ribbon for decoration.

Baking

Place on the middle shelf of a pre-heated oven at 150°C, gas mark 1½, for two to three hours. Use your judgement if you think the oven is too hot, in which case turn it down to 120°C, gas mark ½. After the first hour the ring can be brushed over with soy glaze every twenty minutes until you get the desired colour. When the ring is completely hard, turn off the oven and allow to cool slowly, to avoid any sudden change in temperature and prevent cracking.

Painting and Varnishing

Paint the holly leaves dark green and the berries crimson and the Christmas roses white with yellow centres. Varnish with three coats back and front; when dry make a bow out of some seasonal ribbon and glue on to the holly ring, obscuring the hanging hook.

Greeting Cards 2

Hand-made greeting cards can bring pleasure to both the sender and recipient, especially if the card is for a special occasion. It is possible to buy card blanks from craft suppliers and art shops; these are ready-made cards with envelopes that just need to be decorated. This project demonstrates the versatility of salt dough and how it can be used with other media. As you will only need a small quantity of dough, use the recipe for basic dough and freeze any surplus. The dough motifs can be baked in either a microwave or a conventional oven, and as they are thin they will not take long to dry out. The painting stage is very straightforward and you can use your own colour scheme or the colours I have described as a guide. As an alternative, you can adapt these designs and make refrigerator magnets by using the same modelling and finishing techniques, and sticking a small magnet onto the back of the motif after it has been varnished.

You will need

FOR MODELLING

- Small quantity of basic dough
- Flour for dusting
- Baking parchment
- Flat baking tray
- Sharp knife
- Leaf and blossom cutters

FOR PAINTING

- Water colours
- Gold acrylic
- Paintbrushes
- Card in assorted colours or card blanks
- Paper in assorted colours
- Small square of green felt
- Small scissors or scalpel
- Pencil
- Metal ruler
- Glue
- Envelope

Method

Hearts Roll out some thin dough and use a small cutter to stamp out some heart shapes. The motifs can be air dried and left in an airing cupboard to go hard for about a day, or microwaved on 'low' for twenty minutes, but watch carefully that they do not blister. When the dough is dry, paint with crimson gouache paint and varnish with just one coat. Mount on to a white card 20×8cm (8×3in) with a strip of brown sticky tape down the centre and add some gold acrylic paint and paper stars to finish the pattern.

Holly Wreath With your fingers make two thin sausages of dough 10cm (4in) long, twist them together and join into a ring measuring 5cm (2in) in diameter. Try to make the ring as fine as possible so that it does not weigh too much and add three holly leaves and some berries. Bake at 130°C, gas mark 1, for half an hour and then turn the oven up slightly to brown the ring off. When it has cooled, paint the holly leaves and berries and apply one coat of varnish. Leave the varnish to dry and then make a mount using green felt and gold paper, and attach this on to a piece of red card measuring 14×11cm (5.5×4.5in). When the mount is secure, stick the wreath on with glue.

Summer flowers Roll out a small piece of dough with the rolling pin and stamp out some small leaves and blossoms. To make the tiny roses cut several thin strips of dough and, holding one end between finger and thumb, start to roll it up, fanning the outside edge as you go along. Do not worry if you cannot get the hang of it at first – by the end of the book you will be an expert on making dough roses! Either microwave for twenty minutes on 'low' or put in an oven for one hour at 100–120°C, gas mark ½. When they have cooled, paint the blossoms with a light blue water colour, and leave some of the roses unpainted and add a dab of red with a sponge. Varnish with two coats of matt acrylic varnish and when dry mount on to the card.

TIP:

If you want to post your card, wrap it in tissue paper and send it in a padded jiffy bag.

Basket Plaque

Dough baskets are one of the most traditional salt dough designs seen in books and at craft fairs. Once you have made the basic basket shape you can fill it with all sorts of different fruit, flowers, Easter eggs and even shopping, all modelled out of dough. You can decorate the handle with a small bunch of blossoms to hide the join where the hanging hook is or make a bow out of dough. The hanging hook can be pushed into the back of the main part of the basket, leaving the handle free of any decoration if you prefer. To create a textured finish on the basket base, use two forks held back to back and push them into the dough, making a neat row of small holes with the tines. Another technique is the shortbread effect, which is quite simply a line running from the top of the basket to the bottom and small holes pushed into the dough at intervals to make it look like a piece of shortbread biscuit.

You will need

FOR MODELLING

- One batch of paste dough
- Flour for dusting
- Rolling pin
- Sharp knife
- Water brush
- Two small forks
- Leaf and blossom cutters
- Cheese grater for orange
- Cloves
- Hanging hook
- Baking parchment
- Flat baking tray

FOR PAINTING AND VARNISHING

- Selection of artists' paints
- Fine and medium paintbrushes
- Clear wood varnish

Method

Roll out a piece of dough a 1.5cm (⅔in) thick and use the knife to cut out the shape of the basket base approximately 12cm (5in) wide and 8cm (3in) deep tapering towards the bottom. Place it on the baking parchment and add a small twist of dough to the base of the basket to neaten it off. Press a textured pattern into the dough.

Roll out two pencil-thin pieces of dough approximately 31cm (12in) long with your fingers and twist them together to make the handle. Damp both sides of the basket and attach the handle – you may have to adjust the length and cut off any excess with the knife. Cut the handle in half in the centre, push a small hanging loop in and seal together.

Make some small leaves and blossoms to cover the join on the handle. Decorate the top of the basket base with a selection of leaves in different sizes and add the fruit, making sure that the whole composition looks in proportion (see 'Modelling Fruit').

Baking

Place in a pre-heated oven on the middle shelf at 100–120°C, gas mark ½ for the first hour, then move up to the top shelf for three to four hours.

Painting and Varnishing

Paint the fruit in your chosen colours and leave the basket base natural. Varnish with three coats of clear wood varnish back and front

TIP:

As the basket is made with flat and modelled dough, it will dry out unevenly; this sometimes causes cracks to form after varnishing.
To help prevent this, be sure that the dough is dried right through by checking the back of the model. If there is a dark patch in the centre then it is not ready: return to the oven and leave until thoroughly dry.

Ponies

These rocking ponies make a very popular gift for horse- and pony-mad little girls and even some Mums, too! I usually paint a child's name on the rocker and use it to hang on a bedroom door. They are easily made, and to help you a template is provided here. This project uses wholemeal flour to make the pony because it gives a lovely nutty brown colour; the wholemeal dough is made by the same method as the basic dough recipe. If you want to colour the pony's mane and tail, make up a small amount of black dough (see 'Colouring Dough') using white flour mixed with a teaspoon of black water colour pushed through the garlic press, otherwise leave and paint when baked.

You will need

FOR THE TEMPLATE

- Tracing paper
- Pencil
- Card 16×16cm (6×6in)
- Scalpel/scissors

FOR MODELLING

- One batch of wholemeal basic dough
- Small quantity of black dough
- Flour for dusting
- Rolling pin

- Sharp knife
- Baking parchment
- Flat baking tray
- Pastry brush
- Garlic press
- Hanging loop

FOR PAINTING AND VARNISHING

- Sandpaper
- Selection of artists' paints
- Fine and medium paintbrush
- Clear wood varnish

Method

Roll out the dough to a thickness of 0.5cm (¼in), making sure that the dough is an even thickness and that there are no air bubbles.

Dust the back of the card template with flour and lay it on top of the dough; using a sharp knife, carefully cut around the card, lift the pony cut-out on to some parchment.

Roll out some thin dough and cut out two thin strips to make the bridle and a small patch for the saddle, dampen and attach. Alternatively, leave the pony plain and add a small blossom or ribbon to its mane.

Place a ball of coloured dough in the garlic crusher and push through to make strings of dough for the mane and tail. Drape these on the forehead and neck of the pony in flowing folds and twist together long strands of dough for the tail.

Gently press in the eye and nostril with the pointed end of a paintbrush and add the mouth with the knife. Finally, push in a small hanging loop in the centre of the back underneath the saddle.

Baking

Place on the middle shelf of the oven for the first hour at 100–120°C, gas mark ½. Then move up to the top of the oven for a further three hours until hard.

Painting and Varnishing

Before starting to paint the pony sand off any rough edges. Mark in the eyes with dark blue and the nostrils and mouth in pink. Paint the saddlery in a bright primary colour and add some spots on the pony's flanks. If you are going to write a name on the rocker then mark it out in pencil first, before painting it on with water colour. Varnish with three coats back and front.

TIP:

If you do not feel very confident about painting the name on, use a black felt tip pen.

Pig in Clover

This cheeky piglet standing in a field of clover admiring the view is a must for anyone who collects pigs. You will have enough dough to make several pigs, so fill a trayful; they look fun hanging on a wall together. The dough gives the pig a nice natural colour; just add a few brown or black spots to give him a bit of character.

You will need

FOR MODELLING

- One batch of basic dough

- Flour for dusting

- Baking parchment

- Flat baking tray

- Pastry brush

- Rolling pin

- Sharp knife

- Small blossom cutter

- Metal sieve

- Hanging loop or a paperclip

FOR PAINTING AND VARNISHING

- Water colours

- Fine and medium paintbrushes

- Clear wood varnish

Method

To make the base that the piglet will stand on roll a sausage of dough 10cm (4in) long and 2cm (¾in) thick with your fingers. Place it on a piece of parchment and add some strips of dough to make a fence.

To make the body of the piglet take a ball of dough and press it slightly flat with the palm of your hand to about 8cm (3in). Place the body of the piglet on the dough fence and add four short legs with the hooves cut out so that they are resting on the base.

Take a small ball of dough for the head, dampen and attach to the body, and add a smaller piece of dough, slightly flattened, to make the piglet's snout. Use the pointed end of the paintbrush to press in the nostrils and eyes.

With the rolling pin roll out a thin piece of dough and cut two triangles to make the ears; attach them to the head with a little water. Fold one ear over the eye to give the piglet that cheeky expression. Add a thin coil of dough for the tail and gently press a hanging loop into the back of the piglet.

Make the butterfly with the smallest part of the blossom cutter set. Press out the flower shape in the dough, pinch out one of the petals and fold slightly in the middle. For extra effect add two black stamens for the antennae. Stick the butterfly onto the fence-post using the water.

To make the grass to cover the base, push some dough through the metal sieve, gently lift it off with the knife and arrange it over the damp base. Make the clover leaves by rolling three small balls and flattening them with your finger, stick them together with water into the shape of a leaf and dot around the grass base.

Baking

Place in a pre-heated oven at 100–120°C, gas mark ½, for four to six hours. Move the baking tray to the top shelf after the first hour. Brush the piglet over with water at twenty-minute intervals during the last hour of baking to brown it off.

Painting and Varnishing

Give the piglet some rosy cheeks with a wash of diluted red water colour. Paint one of his ears black or brown and his eyes dark blue. The grass can be painted with a wash of sap green and the clover leaves picked out in a leaf green. When the paint has dried varnish with three coats back and front.

Blue and White Bowl Plaques

These blue and white painted dough bowls where inspired by the patterns on old china plates. This project will need some careful painting and you can get some creative ideas by looking at patterns in books, magazines and on fabrics. Use the template as a guide to make the shape of the bowl, and fill it with a variety of fruit.

You will need

FOR THE TEMPLATE

- Tracing paper
- Pencil
- Card 16cm (6in) square
- Ruler
- Scissors

FOR MODELLING

- Onc batch paste dough
- Flour for dusting
- Baking parchment
- Rolling pin
- Sharp knife
- Water brush
- Hanging loop
- Leaf and blossom cutters
- Black cotton stamens for cherries

FOR PAINTING AND VARNISHING

- Fine and medium artists' paintbrushes
- White acrylic paint
- Selection of water colours
- Clear wood varnish
- Matt acrylic varnish

Method

Make the template by tracing the diagram provided onto the card.

Roll out half the dough to a thickness of 0.5cm (¼in), dust the back of the template with flour and lay it on the dough. Cut around it with the knife and place the bowl plaque on some baking parchment. Add a thin sausage of dough to the top rim of the bowl to add a bit of height and to anchor the hanging loop into, making sure that it does not go into the main body of the plaque as it may cause a crack later on.

Roll out some thin dough, press out eight leaf shapes in different sizes and line the top of the bowl with them. With your fingers model the cherries and strawberries and add them to the bowl (see 'Modelling Fruit').

Baking

Place on a baking tray in a pre-heated oven 100–120°C, gas mark ½, on the middle shelf for four to six hours.

Painting and Varnishing

Sand off any rough edges and paint the bowl with two coats of white or blue acrylic paint depending on the pattern you have chosen. When the base has dried use a fine brush to paint the pattern on. Straight lines can be quite hard to do at first so practise on some paper first and don't overload the brush with paint – make sure you have a fine point on the paintbrush before you start.

TIP:

Make sure that there is no excess water on the dough when it goes into the oven or it may bubble and blister.

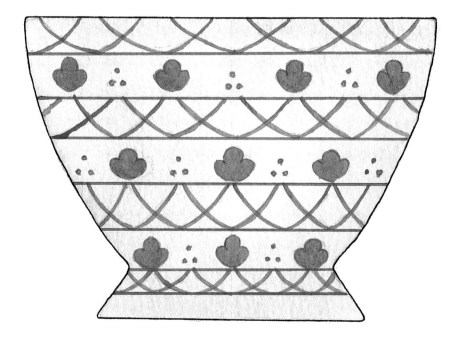

Bouquet of Flowers

Instead of giving flowers that will eventually fade away, why not make them out of dough? By using a combination of coloured and natural dough you can create the feel of abundance by making the flowers in various sizes nestling amongst leaves and stems. It is easier to model the blossoms and leaves out of coloured dough, as painting them afterwards can be quite laborious. For a natural rustic look make a large bouquet of roses with plain dough, using your fingers to model the stems and roses, and add a glaze of egg wash during the last half hour of baking to get a golden brown finish. Small, fine bouquets can be made by using some green strands of dough that have been pushed through the garlic press for stems and the smallest leaf and blossom cutters. To display the bouquet mount it on a hessian-backed frame.

You will need

FOR MODELLING

- One batch of basic dough

- Small quantities of green, red and yellow dough

- Egg glaze (optional)

- Flour for dusting

- Rolling pin

- Small sharp knife

- Leaf and blossom cutter

- Flat baking tray

- Baking parchment

- Hanging loop

- Water brush

FOR PAINTING AND VARNISHING

- ◆ Selection of water colours and acrylics

- ◆ Fine and medium paintbrushes

- ◆ Small piece of sponge

- ◆ Clear satin wood varnish

- ◆ Matt acrylic varnish

Method

To make a base to build your bouquet on roll out a piece of dough to the thickness of 0.5cm (¼in), cut a circle 13cm (5in) in diameter and place it on the baking parchment. Add a narrow rectangle of dough, tapering slightly towards the middle and then fanning out again at the bottom. This is the base which the bouquet will be built upon; place it on some parchment.

With your fingers roll out a dozen thin rolls of green dough and lay them on the base in a disorganized fashion to form the rose stems. Build these up and lay one on top of the other to get some height and dimension.

At this stage insert an 8cm (3in) loop of hanging wire into the top of the dough base so that the top of the loop is showing slightly and the twisted end of the loop is bedded well into the dough.

Roll out a piece of the green dough, press out about a dozen leaf shapes, mark the veins of the leaves with the back of a knife, dampen the backs with the brush and arrange them amongst the stems and around the edge of the base, overlapping on to the parchment.

To make the roses cut ten to fifteen strips of dough of varying sizes, the largest being 2×8cm (1×3in) with either end cut on the diagonal. Holding the strip between finger and thumb, start to roll up the dough like a Swiss roll, gently fanning the outside edge as you go along. Tidy the base of the rose off with the knife, dampen it with a little water and arrange it amongst the stems. Repeat this process until you have covered the tops of stems with roses and they are overflowing on to the parchment Alternate the coloured roses with the plain ones and dot some small blossoms around the edges for contrast.

Making the Bow

Roll out a piece of dough, pastry thin, and cut a rectangle 7×16cm (3×6in). Pinch the middle together with your fingers so that it looks like a butterfly and dampen the outside edges of the rectangle (see page 69). Gather the outside edges one at a time and fold into the centre to make the shape of the bow. Using the back of the knife press the pleats into the bow and then add a small strip of dough across the middle. Cut two ribbons of dough 3×12cm (1×5in) and arrange on the stems, and place the bow so that it is covering the top of the ribbons.

Baking

Place on the baking sheet and put on the top shelf of a pre-heated oven at 100–120°C, gas mark ½, for six to eight hours. Leave to cool slowly in the oven when it has finished baking.

Painting and Varnishing

If you have used coloured dough then just give the red roses a wash of crimson water colour or gouache to deepen the colour and pick out any small blossoms in yellow or white acrylic. Sponge some of the natural roses in crimson to highlight them. Paint the bow with two coats of white acrylic and print a small pattern of dots in red with a very fine paintbrush. Varnish the back of the model with three coats of wood varnish and the front with three coats of matt acrylic to prevent your light colours going yellow

Valentine Hearts

8

This uses a simple twisting tech-nique to make a charming Valen-tine gift. The heart shape is made by joining the two dough twists together using a mitred join. Heart shapes were often used in northern Europe to deco-rate bakers' shop windows, and small biscuit and dough hearts were threaded with coloured wool and used to dress Christmas trees.

You will need

FOR MODELLING

- One batch basic dough
- Flour for dusting
- Baking parchment
- Sharp knife
- Pastry brush
- Hanging loop
- Leaf and blossom cutters

FOR PAINTING AND VARNISHING

- Fine and medium paintbrushes
- Water colours
- White acrylic paint
- Small piece of sponge
- Clear wood varnish

Method

Using your fingers, roll out two sausages of dough 45cm (18in) long and 1cm (½in) thick. Twist them together to make a long, even coil and place it on the lined baking tray.

Gently coax the dough coil into the shape of a heart, cutting the top and bot-tom on a diagonal so that when you join them they fit snugly together, making a mitred join; seal them together with water. Cover the joins with decorations made with leaves and roses.

Baking

Place in a pre-heated oven on the top shelf at 100–120°C, gas mark ½, for three hours, periodically brushing over with water to brown off.

Painting and Varnishing

Paint the roses with white acrylic and sponge on some crimson, and give the leaves a wash of sap green. When the paint is thoroughly dry, varnish with three coats back and front.

Bears

9

Everybody loves a bear, whether it is a cherished and worn soft teddy bear or a china ornamental bear. The teddy bear collectors are passionate about their hobby with shops, exhibitions and magazines dedicated to this addictive pastime. Making dough bears couldn't be easier and you can create a whole selection of bears in different styles and shapes by using your fingers and following simple modelling methods. I have included three different bear designs in this project, the simplest being the bear with the scarf and flowers to hang on the wall. When you have made this bear, you can move on to the studious bear with his book and satchel. The wet weather bear with his yellow sou'wester and red wellies needs a thicker body and longer leg, and will test your modelling skills. The baked dough gives the bears a golden glow so there is no need to paint them unless you want a black or white bear. Make several bears at the same time as they like to have company!

You will need

FOR MODELLING

- ◆ One batch of basic dough

- ◆ Flour for dusting

- ◆ Baking parchment

- ◆ Flat baking tray

- ◆ Rolling pin

- ◆ Sharp knife

- ◆ Hanging loop

- ◆ Cocktail stick

PAINTING AND VARNISHING

- ◆ Water colours

- ◆ White and yellow acrylic paints

- ◆ Fine and medium paintbrushes

- ◆ Clear wood varnish

Method

HANGING BEAR

To make a bear about 16cm (6in) high you will need a ball of dough 7cm (3in). Roll it in the palm of your hand, mould it into an oval shape and place it on a piece of parchment.

Make four sausages of dough with your fingers for the arms and legs. Press creases with the back of the knife at the elbows and knees.

Roll a small ball of dough for the head and attach it to the body with water.

Add a small snout and a round nose, and mark in the mouth with a knife.

Run a seam with the back of the knife from the nose and up in between the ears, and press in the eyes with the top of a paintbrush. Add two crescent-shaped ears modelled with your fingers. When the bear is assembled, carefully add a hanging loop into the back of the head.

SITTING BEAR

To make the bear's body take a well-kneaded ball of dough, mould it into an egg shape and place it on a piece of parchment. Roll out two short sausages of dough with your fingers and cut the ends diagonally so that they fit neatly against the body to make the leg. Turn up the ends to make feet, and press two or three lines with the back of the knife around the knee area.

Add two thinner sausages for the arms and arrange them so that they are resting on the bear's leg, again pressing some lines into the dough where the elbows are. Gently indent a line running from the top of the body down over the bear's tummy to make a seam.

Place the features on the bear's head before attaching it to the body. Push a cocktail stick into the centre of the bear's body, damp the neck area with the brush and gently push the head onto the cocktail stick to secure it to the rest of the body. The cocktail stick will help support the bear and stop the head tilting back in the oven. Finally add scarves, hats, flowers and so on before it goes into the oven.

Baking

Small flat bears will take four to six hours at 100–120°C, gas mark ½. Larger bears sitting up approximately 9cm (3½in) high and weighing 250g (10oz) can be hollowed out with a teaspoon, leaving a crust of 1cm (½in), after the first hour, which will help reduce the baking time to approximately six hours.

Painting and Varnishing

Paint the bear's features with water colours. The bear with the umbrella has been painted with a coat of white acrylic as a base and then two coats of yellow acrylic to finish off the rain mack and hat. The umbrella is painted in black water colour with silver acrylic lines, the wellies and buttons in red crimson acrylic and the trousers in green viridian water colour mixed with white, and then green viridian stripes added afterwards. Varnish with three coats back and front.

Letters

10

A is for apple, B is for bear, C is for cat... Making letters out of dough and decorating them with characters can make a lovely personalized gift for friends and family. For a simple and educational project to make with children, get them to make their own initials and paint them in bright colours. Not all letters are suitable for making initials because they become unbalanced when hung, so you must make sure that the weight is distributed evenly when adding extra characters. Work out first where you are going to put your hanging loop and how you are going to decorate the letter. Alternatively, you can get round this problem by mounting the letter on a hessian-backed frame – these are ready made and available from craft suppliers. A sticky pad added to the back of an initial can also help to keep it straight and stop it from banging if hung on a door.

You will need

FOR MODELLING

- One batch of basic dough
- Flour for dusting
- Flat baking tray
- Baking parchment
- Blossom and leaf cutters
- Cloves
- Hanging loop

FOR PAINTING AND VARNISHING

- Water colours
- White acrylic
- Fine and medium paintbrushes
- Clear wood varnish

Method

LETTER 'A'

With your fingers roll out two sausages of dough about 16cm (6in) long and 3cm (1in) thick. To make the top of the 'A' cut the two ends of the dough sausages diagonally and make a mitred join or corner. Place it on some baking parchment and add a thinner sausage of dough with either end cut diagonally so that it fits snugly across the middle of the 'A'. Press a hanging loop into the top of the letter, tucked underneath so that it is not showing.

Roll out some dough thinly with the rolling pin, press out some leaf shapes with the cutter and arrange them on the letter, covering some of the joins. With your fingers model some small balls to make the apples, push a clove into each one and add them to the leaves. Dot some blossoms around the fruit and at the top of the letter to obscure the hanging loop.

LETTER 'B'

I have used a lower case letter so that I can sit the teddy on it. Make sure that

TIP:

To secure the letters into the hessian display frames, push a pin into the hessian and hook the model onto it. This method is only suitable for lighter letters.

your hanging loop is centred in the back of the long part of the 'b', or it will tip over.

Make the bear by modelling a small ball of dough with your fingers and attaching it to the letter; add four small sausages of dough for the arms and leg. Make the bear's head with its features and ears before attaching it to the body. The honey pot and the bee are made by modelling free style with your fingers.

LETTER 'C'

Place a sausage of dough approximately 30cm (12in) long and 2cm (1in) thick on baking parchment, tidy off the ends and then arrange it in to the shape of a 'C'. Press a paperclip into the top and bottom of the letter to keep it stable when hanging.

Make the cat's body by attaching a ball of slightly flattened dough to the bottom part of the letter. Add a smaller ball for the cat's head, attaching it to the body with water, and add two small flattened balls for the muzzle and a small round nose; press in some whiskers with the knife. Cut out two triangles of dough for the ears and attach. Make the paws by rolling two small sausages of dough and pressing some claws in with the knife. Tuck the end of the leg under the front of the body so that they are overlapping onto the bottom part of the 'C', and add a long, thin coil of dough for the tail. Finally, press in the eyes with the pointed end of a paintbrush.

Add the little mouse by modelling a small ball of dough into a pear shape, add two ears and a long tail, and press in the eyes with a cocktail stick. Attach the mouse to the top of the ' C ' with a dab of water.

Baking

Place the letters on a baking tray on the middle shelf of a pre-heated oven at 120°C, gas mark ½, for the first hour and then move them to the top of the oven for a further two to three hours. Brush letter 'A' with soy glaze towards the end of the baking period to make it golden brown.

Painting and Varnishing

LETTER 'A'

Paint the apples on 'A' with a wash of yellow first. When it has dried, dab some scarlet on with a sponge or the tip of a fine paintbrush. Paint the blossoms in white, and when dry add yellow centres and dab some pink on to the edges of the petals with the sponge.

LETTER 'B'

Letter 'B' is painted with three coats of Hooker's green acrylic and the detail on the bear's tie, yellow with red polka dots and a blue flower. Leave the honey pot unpainted, highlighting the lid in gold acrylic. I used a very fine paintbrush to write on the honey pot with; if you do not feel very confident about writing with a brush, then use a fine black felt tip pen.

LETTER 'C'

The cat is painted in velvet gouache with a white acrylic tail. Paint the mouse in a watery grey with a black nose and pink tail. Mix some yellow acrylic with crimson to get a scarlet to paint the 'C' with, and add some lemon yellow dots as a pattern.

Poppy Ring

T his colourful dough ring with poppies and ears of corn conjures up memories of harvest time and long summer days in the country. The ring is 26cm (10in) in diameter and this design can be used as a base for other fruit and flower themes. The poppies are made using the largest cutter of a set of blossom cutters (see page 29), or you can use small balls of dough flattened with your fingers into petal shapes. Make some red dough using scarlet poster colour or gouache. The black poppy centres are made by pushing some black dough through a fine metal sieve. The poppy-and-corn design can also be used to decorate bowls and baskets.

You will need

FOR MODELLING

- Two batches of basic dough

- Small quantities of green, red and black dough

- Flour for dusting

- Soy glaze

- Flat baking tray 30×30cm (12×12in)

- Baking parchment

- Set of three blossom and leaf cutters

- Small pair of nail scissors

- Water brush

- Metal sieve

- Sharp knife

- Hanging loop

FOR PAINTING AND VARNISHING

- Selection of water colours and acrylics

- Fine and medium paintbrushes

- Clear wood varnish

Method

Roll out two long coils of dough 60cm (24in) long and 3cm (1in) thick with your fingers; lay them next to each other and check that they are the same width, and smooth all the way down. Then twist them together until you have an even rope of dough, and carefully lift it onto a lined baking tray, arrange in a circle about 26cm (10in) and cut off any excess. Push a long piece of hanging loop well into the dough and join the two ends of the ring together with water. Cover the ring with a tea towel to prevent it drying out while you are making the decorations.

Roll out some green dough, press out twenty leaf shapes in different sizes and arrange them on the ring, covering the join at the top where the hanging loop is and at the bottom and the sides.

To make the ears of corn roll about twenty small sausages of dough with

your fingers, between 3cm and 6cm (1in and 2in) long. Snip the dough diagonally up and down with the scissors (see page 14). Dampen the leaves and arrange the ears of corn over them, so that they overlap on to the ring.

To make the poppies roll out the red dough and, using the largest blossom cutter, press out about fourteen shapes (see 'Modelling Fruit and Flowers'). Then, holding the blossom in your hand, carefully damp the edges of each petal with water using a small paintbrush and join each to its neighbour until you have formed the poppy. Damp the backs and arrange them around the corn.

Take a small ball of black dough and push it through the sieve using a wooden spoon. Moisten the centre of the poppies with a little water, and with the damp tip of the knife gently lift off enough black dough to place in the centre of each.

Finally, roll out a small ball of plain dough using the smallest blossom cutter, press out fourteen shapes and dot them around the poppies.

Baking

Place the poppies in the centre of a pre-heated oven at 120°C, gas mark ½, for the first hour, then move them up to the top shelf and turn the oven up by 10° for a further three to four hours. Brush the ring over with soy glaze during the last hour of baking.

Painting and Varnishing

Paint the small blossoms white with yellow centres and give the poppies just a wash of crimson to deepen the colour. Varnish with three coats back and front.

Tip:

Wear thin protective rubber or plastic gloves when varnishing large pieces so that you can pick them up to varnish underneath.

Delivery Girl

12

This little dough girl carrying her loaves of bread uses a simple method of building and modelling the figure using your fingers. The model is assembled rather like a peg doll using a sausage of dough for the body, a small ball for the head and flat rolled-out sheets of dough for the clothes. This method can be adapted to make most flat figures for hanging on walls. The arms can be left hanging down on either side of the body or folded in front, holding an object. Once they have been held in place with a little water they will set into that shape in the oven. It is important that all figures are baked slowly because the different layers will dry out unevenly and can crack if the baking process is too hot. This quantity of dough will make two figures approximately 16cm (6in) high and weighing about 225g (8oz).

You will need

FOR MODELLING

- One batch of basic dough
- Small quantity of coloured dough for clothes (optional)
- Flour for dusting
- Flat baking tray or wire cooling tray
- Baking parchment
- Rolling pin
- Water brush
- Sharp knife
- Garlic press
- Wire hanging loop

FOR PAINTING

- Selection of water colours and acrylics
- Fine and medium paintbrushes
- Clear wood varnish

Method

With your fingers, roll a ball of well-kneaded dough into a sausage about 30cm (12in) long and the thickness of a finger. Place it on the baking parchment and double it over to form the body. Add a small ball of dough for the head and attach it to the top of the body with a dab of water. Make the overall length of the girl about 16cm (6in) and trim off any excess dough.

Roll out some dough with the rolling pin to the thickness of thin pastry crust and use the knife to cut out the shape of the skirt – you do not have to be very precise as long as the dough is smooth and there are no fine cracks in it. Drape the skirt over the body, turning under the sides and leaving enough room at the top to add the arms and collar.

Add two thin sausages of dough for the arms, making one slightly longer than the other because it has to hold the

Dough figures can be baked on a wire cooling tray to speed the drying process along, but make sure you keep the figure on the baking parchment.

loaves of bread, and cut the top ends at a diagonal so that they fit neatly against the body. Roll out a thin piece of dough, cut out the collar and attach it to the body, covering the tops of the arms and the skirt.

To make the loaves roll two small sausages of dough with your fingers, taper them at either end and make some marks across the top with the back of the knife; then wrap them in a small square of thin dough as if they have just come out of the patisserie! Gently lay the bread over the body of the dough girl, arrange the arms around it and secure it with a little water. Roll two pea-sized balls of dough for the hands and press in some lines for fingers with the knife. Add two strips of thin dough for cuffs to cover the joins where the hands are attached to the arms.

Press in the features on the face using the end of the paintbrush for the eyes, add a smiling mouth with the knife and use a small dent or ball of dough for the nose. With the water brush, lightly damp the area on the head where the hair is to go. Push a ball of dough through the garlic press, take some of the strands with your fingers and arrange them so that they drape and curl over the shoulders of the girl; add some shorter bits to make a fringe.

Finally, carefully push the twisted end of the hanging loop into the back of the head and place on the flat baking tray.

Baking

Place the dough girl in the middle of a pre-heated oven at 100°C, gas mark ½, for the first hour, then move her up to the top shelf for five hours until baked through. Brush the figure's face and hands over with a little water to encourage the dough to plump out.

Painting and Varnishing

Sand off any rough edges around the shirt and collar and paint in the features on the face; add two rosy cheeks with a little red water colour. If you want to decorate the skirt with a pattern, then cover it with two coats of acrylic and add the pattern when it has dried. Varnish with three coats back and front.

TIP:

These dough dollies can be personalized by painting a child's name on the skirt and hanging it on a bedroom door. A keen cook or bread-maker might appreciate a dough dolly with his or her name on it to decorate the kitchen.

Step by Step

Diagram of dough dolly in different stages.

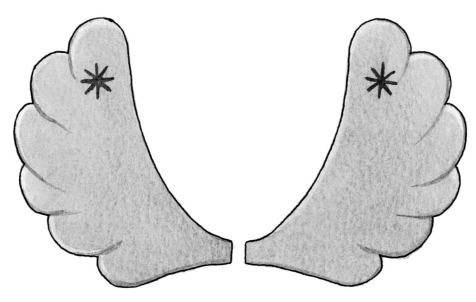

Angels

13

Once you have got the hang of making dough figures these angels are very straightforward. Use the template provided to make the wing or just cut out a set free hand. The larger angels are approximately 17cm (6½in) tall and weigh 175g (6oz): you may find that they are rather heavy to hang on a Christmas tree and are more suited to decorate a wall. The smaller angels weigh 100g (4oz) and can hang on the top of tree. I have used a twist of copper picture-hanging wire to make the halos for the small angels and a twist of dough for the larger ones. Create starburst patterns on the angels' wings and gowns using a star-shaped icing nozzle and the beading effect with the lemon zester.

You will need

FOR THE TEMPLATE

- Tracing paper
- Piece of card
- Pencil
- Scissors

FOR MODELLING

- One batch of basic dough
- Flour for dusting
- Rolling pin
- Sharp knife

- Garlic press
- Lemon zester
- Star-shaped piping nozzle
- Copper wire for halo
- Water brush
- Baking parchment
- Flat baking tray or wire cooling rack
- Hanging loop
- Thin ribbon

FOR PAINTING

- Fine and medium paintbrushes
- Bonze and white acrylic paint
- Selection of water colours and gouache paints
- Small piece of sponge
- Clear wood varnish
- Soluble matt acrylic varnish for white and pastel colours

Method

SMALL ANGEL

Trace the wing template on to card, cut it out and dust the back with flour. Roll a small ball of dough out to a thickness of 0.5cm (¼in) and place the template on it. Carefully cut around the edge of the template to make one wing, then reverse it to make the second. Place the wing on some parchment, trim the two bottom ends and join them with a little water.

Roll a small ball of dough in your fingers to make the head, damp the back and place it over the join where the two wings meet. Roll a sausage of dough 20cm (8in) long and 1cm (½in) in diameter, and assemble the angel's body (see page 85) making the overall length about 13cm (5in) including the head. Damp the head with the water brush and add some dough hair.

Press some patterns into the skirt using the piping nozzle and lemon zester, and add a twist of copper wire for a halo and a small hanging loop or paperclip.

LARGE ANGEL

Use the same size wing template, but do not trim the bottom ends as they need to be slightly bigger this time. Join them and place them on the baking parchment.

Assemble the angel (see page 85), remembering to make the arms a little longer so that they can be folded in front of the body to hold a hymn book or holly wreath.

To make the angel's hair into ringlets cut a rectangle of thin dough large enough to cover the head and shoulders. Cut long strips on either side of the rectangle and make some shorter strips for a fringe. Place it on the angel's head, brush over lightly with the water brush and then with your fingers gently twist each strip of dough into a ringlet. Add the hanging loop before the model is ready to go into the oven.

Baking

Place the models on a flat baking tray or wire cooling rack on the middle shelf of a pre-heated oven at 100–120°C, gas mark ½, for the first hour. Then they can be moved up to the top shelf of the oven, the small angels for a further three to four hours and the large angels for six to eight hours. Leave them to cool slowly in the oven after baking.

Painting and Varnishing

Highlight the angels' wing tips with bronze acrylic dabbed on with the sponge and the stars and beading with a paintbrush. As it seems traditional for angels to be either white or pastel coloured you can use a water colour varnish to prevent yellowing. Finish off by threading some thin gold ribbon through the hanging loop.

TIP

If it is more convenient, the models can be baked overnight. Turn the oven down to its lowest setting, usually 80–90°C, gas mark ¼, or 'minimum'. This is when Agas come into their own as the models can be left in the warming oven for hours.

Witches

Hallowe'en can conjure up all sorts of inspiring ideas for things to make with dough, from a simple round pumpkin to a witch or a wizard. Use the basic step-by-step method of assembling the figure as described in the previous projects. For this project I have used some black- and brown-coloured dough for the witches' clothes and green dough for the small witch's hair. You can add a broom handle made of twig with the brush made from dough pushed through the garlic press, or use a bit of free style modelling to make a cat sitting at the witch's feet.

You will need

FOR MODELLING

- One batch of basic dough

- Brown-, black- and green-coloured dough (see 'Colouring Dough')

- Flour for dusting

- Small, sharp knife

- Rolling pin

- Water brush

- Flat baking tray

- Baking parchment

- Star-shaped piping nozzle

- Lemon zester

- Garlic press

- Thin piece of twig for a wand

- Hanging loop

FOR PAINTING AND VARNISHING

- Fine and medium paintbrushes

- Gold acrylic paint

- Selection of water colours

- Clear wood varnish

Method

Start by making the witch's cloak by rolling out a piece of black dough as thin as pastry crust. Cut out a rough oval shape large enough to assemble the witch on and with enough black dough showing on either side to press in a star pattern. Place it on a piece of baking parchment.

Make the witch using the basic dough figure technique. Roll out some brown dough, cut the shape of the gown out, drape it over the body and press in a beaded pattern with the lemon zester around the edge of the skirt. Add two sausages of dough for the arms, making them slightly wider at the cuff ends. Attach two pea-sized balls with fingers marked out for the hands and neaten off by adding two strips of dough for the cuffs with the beading pattern pressed in before you put them on to the end of the arms. Make a collar of black dough and

attach it to the top of the gown, covering the joins of the arms. At this stage, press the hanging hook into the back of the head.

To make the pumpkin roll a small piece of dough into a ball with your fingers and press some lines into it with the back of the knife. Arrange it on the witch's body and wrap the arm and hand around part of it. Add a small piece of twig for a wand and push one end into the dough, wrapping the witch's other hand around the base of the twig.

To make the hat, first roll out a piece of black dough and cut a semicircle out with either a small cookie cutter or the knife to make the brim, arrange it on the witch's head and trim off any excess. Then cut a triangle of dough out to make the top of the hat and attach it to the brim with water. Push the triangle together with your fingers to make it into a cone shape. Place the witch on the baking tray and transfer to the oven.

Baking

Place on the middle shelf in a pre-heated oven at 100°C, gas mark ½, for the first hour then move up to the top shelf for a further four to five hours. Allow to cool slowly in the oven after baking has finished. Depending on the size and thickness of your witch, you may find that the baking time takes longer. Always tap the back of the model to test if it is baked through.

Painting and Varnishing

Paint the features on the witch's face, the stars and the beading with gold acrylic, and the pumpkin with an orange water colour. Add the detail on the pumpkin with a fine paintbrush and finish off with three coats of varnish back and front, allowing each coat to dry thoroughly.

The Shepherd

15

This dough shepherd will test your modelling skills as he is chunkier than the dough girls and his body is made with two thicker rolls of dough, one for the top half of the body and another modelled into the waist and legs. Use this technique to make descriptive scenes using other characters such as a golfer holding a set of clubs or a cricketer, footballer or rugby player.

You will need

FOR MODELLING

- One batch of basic dough

- Flour for dusting

- Flat baking tray

- Baking parchment

- Rolling pin

- Sharp knife

- Water brush

- Garlic press

- Fine wire sieve

- Small blossom cutter

- Thin piece of twig 13cm (5in) long for the shepherd's crook

FOR PAINTING AND VARNISHING

- Fine and medium paintbrushes

- Selection of water colours and acrylics

- Clear wood varnish

Method

To start with, make the base that the shepherd is going to stand on by rolling a thick sausage of dough with your fingers about 13cm (5in) long and place it on the baking parchment. Roll out a thinner piece of dough, cut four narrow strips for the fencing, damp and attach it to one side of the base.

Assemble the shepherd's body by taking a ball of dough and making it into the shape of the torso 7cm (2½in) from neck to waist and 7cm (2½in) across the chest. Model the bottom half and the leg in a similar way, and attach to the base after adding two round balls of dough for shoes.

Make a ball of dough for the head, damp the neck area and attach the head to the body. A cocktail stick can be used to reinforce the support between the head and the body. Add the arms and hands with cuffs and start to make the shepherd's clothes out of thin pieces of dough cut into the shape of a waistcoat and trousers. Press creases and wrinkles in the trousers with the back of the knife. Make small pockets for the waistcoat and add a thin piece of dough for a handkerchief. Press in any detail such as stitching or buttonholes with the knife, and add the hanging hook, pushed firmly into the base of the wood.

Make the hat by cutting a semicircle of thin dough for the brim, and place it on the head with the front turned up over the model's eyes. Then add a wide strip of dough for the top of the hat and a small piece for the crown – you may have to practise a bit to get this right. Push a little dough through the sieve to make some hair and add it to the shepherd's head so that it is showing under the hat. Mark in the eyes and mouth, and add a small ball of dough for the nose.

To make the sheep, roll a small ball of dough with your fingers, flatten it slightly and add two thin sausages of dough for the front legs. Attach it to the dough base and the side of the shepherd's leg. Push some dough through the metal sieve to make the fleece. Add an almond-shaped piece of dough for the head, and some ears, and press in the eyes and nostrils with the end of a cocktail stick.

Take the long piece of twig and arrange it against the shepherd's body with his hand wrapped around it. Add a piece of dough onto the top of the twig to make the hook; you may find that this is difficult to keep in place, so it can be baked separately and then stuck onto the twig with glue.

Finally, add any extra detail such as buttons, grass and flowers to the model and transfer it to a flat baking tray.

Baking

Place on the middle shelf in a preheated oven at 100–120°C, gas mark ½, for up to eight hours. As this model is quite thick it might be more convenient to bake it overnight. Leave to cool slowly in the oven after it has finished baking.

Painting and Varnishing

Use a yellow acrylic mixed with white to paint the shirt, and when it is dry add some red checks using crimson and a very fine paintbrush. As you will need a steady hand for this, practise first on a piece of paper. The waistcoat is painted with two coats of hooker's green acrylic and the trousers in red alzirian goauche. Leave the sheep unpainted, marking the eyes and nostrils with black water colour. Varnish back and front with three coats.

Door Key Hanger 16

This can make a fun house-warming present; the tradition of giving bread and salt as a welcoming gesture goes back many centuries and is used in Arab countries to this day. A gift made of salt dough is the modern equivalent and keeps the tradition of bringing luck and good fortune to a new household alive. For a personal touch you could paint the house number on the door and choose a relevant colour scheme. The hen and her two chicks can be adapted for hanging tea towels or oven gloves in the kitchen. Push two small paperclips into the back of the model before baking and then thread a thin piece of ribbon through to hang it with. Make sure that it is hung away from a kettle or a sink where it may get damp. Use yacht varnish for this project as it will give your model added protection against knocks and chips.

- Two short twigs
- Star-shaped piping nozzle
- Water brush
- Small brass cup hooks (from DIY stores)
- Large paperclip/hanging loop
- Flat baking tray

FOR PAINTING AND VARNISHING

- Selection of acrylic paints
- Water colours
- Fine and medium paintbrushes
- Clear yacht varnish

You will need

FOR MODELLING

- One batch of paste dough
- Small quantity of green-coloured dough
- Flour for dusting
- Baking parchment
- Rolling pin
- Sharp knife
- Ruler

Method

To make the door, roll out a piece of dough 0.5cm (¼in) thick, use the ruler to mark out a rectangle approximately 6x14cm (3½x5½in), cut it out and place it on the baking parchment. Roll out a sausage of dough with your fingers the same width as the door and attach at the base to make a door step. Mark in the door panels with the back of the knife, add a door knob and a knocker, and push the paperclip into the top of the door for a hanging hook.

Using your fingers, model two plant pots, marking the rims of the pots with the back of the knife. To make the top of

the trees, push some green dough through the piping nozzle and form two circles, carefully push the piece of twig into the pot base and add the green dough on to the top of the twig to make the tree. Repeat the process for the second tree and attach it to the sides of the door, making sure that you damp the dough with the water brush so that it bonds securely. Finally, add some small balls of dough to represent fruit.

Add other details such as a milk bottle, newspaper and cat by modelling with your fingers. Push two cup hooks into the bottom of the door just before it goes into the oven – the heat of the baking process will bond around the hooks and hold them securely in place.

Baking

Transfer the model on to the baking tray and place on the middle shelf of a pre-heated oven at 100–120°C, gas mark ½, for one hour, then move it up to the top shelf for a further four hours. Check that the hooks haven't moved during the first hour of baking. Leave to cool in the oven.

Painting and Varnishing

Paint your door in a matt acrylic with a gold or bronze door-knocker and knob. Leave the newspaper in plain dough and with a very fine paintbrush or black felt tip pen mark in lines to simulate printing. For other details use the illustration as a guide and when the paint is dry varnish with three coats back and front.

Decorative Gift Boxes

U sing salt dough to add a relief decoration on to flat objects is a very easy and effective way of producing an inexpensive and professional-looking gift that is also useful. Box blanks made of papier mâché or wood are easily available these days by mail order from most craft suppliers. If you want to create a fruit or flower theme, then use the techniques already covered. Other themes can include the sun, moon and stars using cookie cutters or brightly coloured balls and squares of dough modelled to look like sweets. You will need to paint the box to blend in with the design on the lid; generally, some acrylic water-based paint applied with a sponge will provide a good matt covering. Add different finishing effects with gold or bronze dabbed on with a sponge, or add a pattern of dots or flowers. You can apply this design technique to decorate other useful gift ideas like the note pad illustrated on page 24.

You will need

FOR MODELLING

- Small quantity of basic dough
- Flour for dusting
- Leaf cutters
- Cloves
- Small cones
- Cheese grater for oranges and lemons
- Water brush
- Sharp knife
- Baking parchment
- Plain wood or cardboard box blanks (see List of Suppliers)

FOR PAINTING AND VARNISHING

- Selection of water colours and acrylics
- Fine and medium paintbrushes for detail on fruit
- Wide paintbrush for painting the boxes
- Sponge or piece of rag
- Gold and bronze acrylic for highlighting
- Clear wood varnish
- Strong glue

Method

Roll out a flat piece of dough and press out several leaf shapes. Mark in the veins with the back of the knife and arrange on a piece of parchment.

With your fingers model the pears, apples, oranges, lemons and so on (see 'Modelling Fruit and Flowers') and add them to the leaf base, arranging them in a neat cluster. Add the cones and transfer the decoration onto the baking sheet.

Baking

Place in a pre-heated oven on the top shelf at 100–120°C, gas mark ½, for one to two hours. This project can be air dried if the decorations aren't too thick.

Painting and Varnishing

THE BOX

While the decoration is baking, paint the fruit and cone box blank with a wash of brown water colour. Use wide brush marks and then drag the paintwork gently with the rag to give it a distressed look. When the brown has dried, sponge on some gold or bronze acrylic. Sponge some pale green acrylic on to the orange and lemon box, and when it has dried add a pattern of small white dots with a fine paintbrush.

THE FRUIT

Paint the fruit and leaves, and when dry, varnish with a couple of coats. Finally, attach the dough decoration to the box lid with strong glue.

Easter Egg Basket

T his basket is ideal for collecting Easter eggs in or serving hot cross buns at teatime. It can also make a gift for a chocoholic filled with chocolate eggs and wrapped in cellophane or tissue, and dressed with a ribbon. I have used a lattice pastry cutter to make the base; if you haven't got a cutter then use thin strips of dough in a criss-cross pattern instead. Other bowl rim decorations can include flowers and fruit and should always be added after the bowl is hard enough to stand unsupported in the oven.

You will need

FOR MODELLING

◆ One batch of paste dough

◆ Flour for dusting

◆ Lattice pastry cutter

◆ Sharp knife

◆ Rolling pin

◆ Fine metal sieve

◆ Blossom and leaf cutters

◆ Baking parchment/foil

◆ Oven-proof bowl without a rim, about 16cm (6in) in diameter

FOR PAINTING AND VARNISHING

◆ Acrylics

◆ Fine and medium paintbrushes

◆ Small piece of sponge

◆ Yacht varnish for pieces that are not going to used for food

Method

Make sure that the dough is well kneaded and pliable, then roll it out on a well-floured surface until you have a wide enough sheet, the thickness of pastry crust, to cover the mould. Using the pastry lattice cutter, mark out the pattern on the dough. Turn the mould upside down and wrap the baking parchment around it, tucking any excess paper or foil under the mould, and place the mould on the lined baking tray.

Roll out two thin sausages of dough and twist them together to make a rim, then arrange them around the lip of the upturned mould. This will be the rim of the dough bowl when it is turned the right way up. Damp the edges of the rim with water, ready for the dough lattice to be attached (see page 27). Lay the sheet of dough over the mould and use the knife or sharp scissors to trim off any excess dough, making sure that the base is securely attached to the rim.

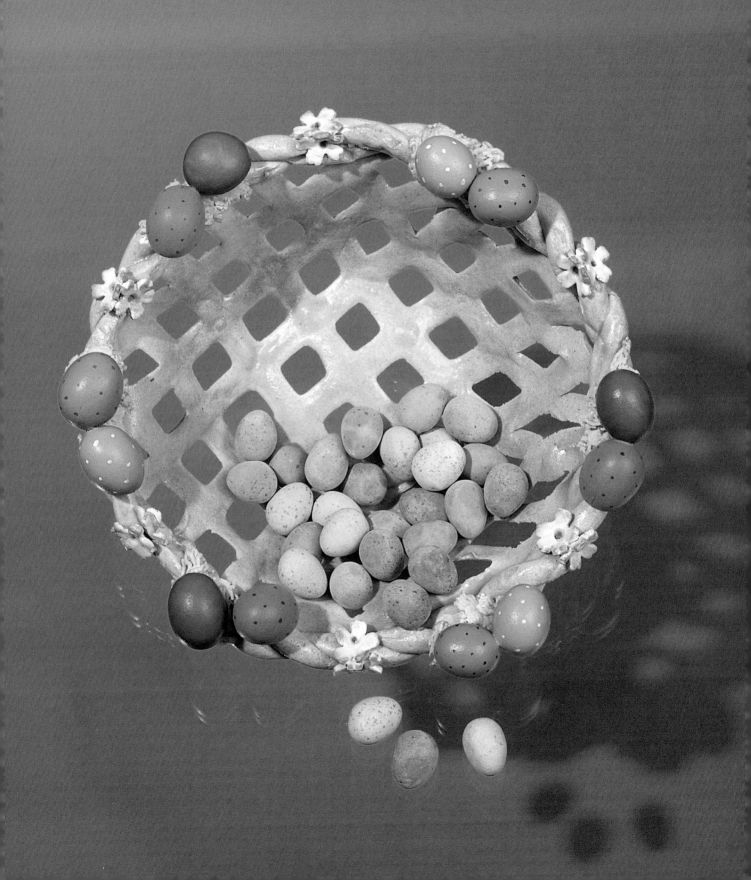

When the basket has been baked (see below), make the eggs by rolling twelve even-shaped balls of dough and put to one side while you make up a little paste of dough mixed with water. Use this to stick the dough straw and eggs on to the rim. Add some small blossoms to finish off the decoration, return to the oven and leave for one to two hours until baked.

Baking

Place in a pre-heated oven near the top at 120°C, gas mark ½, until the basket is firm enough to take off the mould, about two to three hours. Alternatively, microwave in two twenty-minute bursts on 'defrost' then two ten-minute bursts on 'low', but keep an eye on it because it may bubble and blister. When the basket is firm enough to stand on its own, slip off the mould, turn the right way up and add the decoration on the rim, as described in the previous paragraph.

Painting and Varnishing

I have used white acrylic mixed with scarlet water colour to make the matt terracotta pink egg, and viridian green water colour mixed with white again to get the verdigris and turquoise colour. When the eggs have dried paint some polka dots in contrasting colours on them using a very fine paintbrush. Finally, varnish the bowls with a yacht varnish if they are going to be used for decorative purposes. I tend to leave bowls that are to be used for food because of the possibility of the varnish causing a taint. Protect the bowls from grease by lining them with a napkin and store somewhere warm when not in use.

TIP:

If you are using foil to cover the mould with, remember not to put it in the microwave.

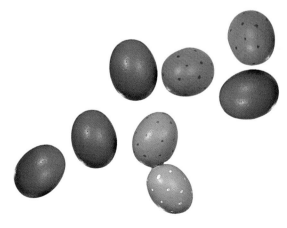

Candle Holder

19

This plaited candle holder looks as if it is made out of carved wood. The honey tones of the dough would complement a pine dining table or a plain wooden mantelpiece. Recently while I was browsing through a craft magazine I discovered that certain craft suppliers stock brass candle cups which can be pushed into the dough before baking and as a result will provide a secure holder for the candle. If you want to protect the dough from dripping wax, use non-drip candles, although the wax is quite easy to remove and will not damage the dough. You can also use this technique to make a decorative plait for the wall. Make a loop of dough at one end, add a bow (see page 69), decorate with your chosen fruit and paint the ribbon to match the colour scheme of the room.

You will need

FOR MODELLING

- Two batches of basic dough
- Flour for dusting
- Soy or egg glaze
- Flat baking tray 30×30cm (12×12in)
- Baking parchment
- Rolling pin
- Sharp knife
- Leaf cutter
- Cloves
- Water brush
- Ruler
- Brass candle cups (see List of Suppliers)

FOR PAINTING AND VARNISHING

- Gloss yacht varnish
- Felt or cork for backing
- Glue

Method

With your fingers roll out three long sausages of dough approximately 56cm (22in) long and 3cm (1in) thick. Place them on a well-floured surface, join them together with a little water at one end and start to plait, making sure that the ropes of dough are not getting stretched (see page 24). When you have a nice, even plait, transfer it onto the lined baking tray; if the plait is longer than the baking tray, cut excess dough off with the knife.

Use the ruler to measure three equal points as a guide to where to place the candle cups in the dough. Insert the candle cups and then moisten the rest of the plait to stop it drying out while you are preparing the leaves and fruit (see page 29).

Arrange the leaves and fruit along the plait, add a ring of dough around each candle cup and decorate with some small roses and berries.

Baking

Place on the top shelf of a pre-heated oven at 100–120°C, gas mark ½. After the first hour turn the oven up slightly for another three to four hours. When the plait is hard enough to move, gently lift it off the baking tray and place it directly onto the oven shelf. If you want to deepen the colour of the baked dough, brush it over with egg or soy glaze during the last hour of baking. Allow the plait to cool slowly in the oven before removing it.

Painting and Varnishing

Decorate in your chosen colours or leave unpainted, and varnish with three coats back and front. To protect your table surface from any possible damage, line the underside of the plait with a strip of felt or cork tile.

Mirror Frames

20

Salt dough as a medium for bonding mirror and glass really comes into its own when making mirror frames. Follow the step-by-step instructions set out below and make a special mirror for every occasion. I would not recommend making anything too big, as time and damp may weaken the frame if it is heavy. Always use paste dough for added strength and place the frame with its mirror in a cold oven so that it warms up slowly. This quantity of dough will make two mirror frames approximately 13cm (5in) in diameter.

You will need

FOR MODELLING

- One batch paste dough
- Flour for dusting
- Mirror 2mm thick cut to required shape, or mirror tiles
- Saucer 15cm (6in) in diameter
- Heart-shaped cutter
- Set of leaf and blossom cutters
- Calyx or small star-shaped cutter
- Hanging hook
- Star-shaped piping nozzle
- Ruler
- Rolling pin
- Water brush
- Parchment
- Flat baking tray

FOR PAINTING AND VARNISHING

- Acrylic water based verdigris kit for bronzing effect (see List of Suppliers)
- Gold and bronze acrylic in tube form (Daler Rowney)
- Crimson designers' gouache (Daler Rowney)
- Small piece of sponge
- Medium and fine paintbrushes
- Satin clear polyurethane wood varnish

Method

HEART MIRROR

Roll a small ball of dough into a sausage 26cm (10in) long. Arrange it in a circle and gently roll flat with the rolling pin to make a ring about 13cm (5in) in diameter. Insert the hanging loop into the top of the ring, ready to be covered by the mirror. Place on the parchment and brush over with a little water, then put the round mirror 12cm (4½in) in diameter onto the ring base and push it down gently, so that it is bedded into the dough

Roll out a sheet of dough the thickness of pastry crust and, using a saucer as a template, cut a circle of dough and lay it over the mirror. Seal the edges around the mirror using your fingers and cut away any excess dough, so that you are left with a neat circle.

Dust the heart-shaped cutter with flour and use it to cut out a shape in the centre of the mirror. Roll a long thin sausage of dough with your fingers to make the border around the edge of the mirror, and use the back of the knife to make diagonal marks so that it looks as though the dough has been twisted. Finally, using a well-floured piping nozzle, press a pattern gently into the dough. Transfer onto the baking tray ready to go into the oven.

BRONZED MIRROR

Prepare the mirror base as above and add a 31cm (12in) sausage of dough for the frame around the mirror. Damp the base and the edge of the glass and gently press the frame onto it, cutting off any excess dough and making sure that the frame and base are sealed together. Decorate with leaves, roses and small blossoms. Transfer to the baking tray.

STAR FLOWER MIRROR

Roll out a flat piece of dough 0.5cm (¼in) thick, place the square mirror measuring 13×13cm (5×5in) on the dough and cut around it with a knife, leaving a margin of 0.5cm (¼in); you can use a ruler as a guide. Lift the mirror off, cut a circle of dough out of the base, damp it, return the mirror and push gently down to secure it in place.

Measure the sides of the dough base and roll out four sausages of dough the thickness of a finger to make the frame. Cut each end on the diagonal to make mitred joins or corners, damp the base and attach the frame one side at a time, making sure that it is overlapping the edge of the glass. Use the back of the knife to score diagonal lines on the frame and add some star shapes and small balls of dough for a final decoration.

Baking

Place mirrors on the middle shelf in a cold oven, then allow to heat up to 100–120°C, gas mark ½, and leave to bake for three to four hours. When the frames are hard turn off the oven and allow to cool slowly.

Painting and Varnishing

HEART

With the sponge dab on some crimson gouache thinly so that it highlights the star pattern. Paint the border with either bronze or gold acrylic. Varnish with three coats, making sure that the back of the mirror is well covered and taking care around the edges of the heart cut-out.

BRONZED MIRROR

Follow the paint manufacturer's instructions for applying the different stages of this bronzing/verdigris technique. I find it easier to varnish the frame first and, when it is dry, apply the paint finish so that the full effect of this technique may be appreciated.

STAR FLOWER MIRROR

I have used a matt acrylic hobby paint for the frame. Paint the flowers in white acrylic and add detail with a fine paintbrush. Varnish as above.

TIPS:

To prevent any unpainted dough being reflected in the glass, the frame can be made out of dark-coloured dough.

Mask the glass with paper before varnishing.

The backs of the mirrors can be finished off by lining them with thin cork floor tile or felt.

List of Suppliers

For box blanks and craft accessories:

Janik Ltd
Brickfield Lane
Denbigh Road
RUTHIN
Denbigshire
LL15 2TN

Tel: 01824 702096
Fax: 01824 707383

For specialist paint finishes:

Mad Hatters
8 High Street
OTFORD
Kent
TN14 5PQ

Tel: 01959 525578

For card blanks:

Craft Creations Ltd
Ingersol House
Delamare Road
CHESNUT
Herts
EN8 9ND

Tel: 01992 781900
Fax: 01992 634339

**For specialist cookie cutters
and accessories:**

Foxrun Craftsmen Ltd
Fox House
Stonedale Road
STONEHOUSE
GL10 3SA

Tel: 01453 828333

Index